To Bob + Kathy,

Best wishes
and good celebrations!

Andrea Reye

5/21/09

CELEBUTARDS

Celebutards

☆

Hollywood Hacks, Limousine Liberals,
Pandering Politicians Who Are
Destroying America!

ANDREA PEYSER

CITADEL PRESS
Kensington Publishing Corp.
www.kensingtonbooks.com

CITADEL PRESS BOOKS are published by

Kensington Publishing Corp.
850 Third Avenue
New York, NY 10022

All Kensington titles, imprints, and distributed lines are available at special quantity discounts for bulk purchases for sales promotions, premiums, fund-raising, educational, or institutional use. Special book excerpts or customized printings can also be created to fit specific needs. For details, write or phone the office of the Kensington special sales manager: Kensington Publishing Corp., 850 Third Avenue, New York, NY 10022, attn: Special Sales Department; phone 1-800-221-2647.

First printing: February 2009

10 9 8 7 6 5 4 3 2 1

Printed in the United States of America

Library of Congress Control Number: 2008936725

ISBN-13: 978-0-8065-3109-0
ISBN-10: 0-8065-3109-6

For Mark and Eliza Rose

CONTENTS

CONTENTS

FOREWORD:
What, No
Conservatives?

A NUMBER OF LIBERAL-MINDED FRIENDS suggested that I include a few right-wing celebs in this book. The name that came up most frequently was that of Ann Coulter, a woman whom I like and respect a great deal.

Yes, Coulter criticized several New Jersey women who lost their husbands in the 9/11 terrorist attacks as "enjoying" their husbands' deaths in her 2006 book *Godless: The Church of Liberalism*. However, Coulter is not the first writer to forthrightly speak her mind. Two years earlier, Dorothy Rabinowitz penned a column in the *Wall Street Journal* that took to task four so-called "Jersey Girls" for exploiting their mates' 9/11 deaths for the benefit of the Democratic Party, a theme that has been repeated by other writers, including myself. The sentiment simply did not ignite nearly as much uproar as when the conservative firebrand took on the widows.

I consider myself to the right of center politically. I support classic conservative causes, such as crime-fighting, tax-cutting, welfare reform, and the death penalty, but I'm live-and-let-live on a variety of social issues, including abortion and gay rights. As a result, some of my fellow New Yorkers consider me a raving right-winger, while others who discover my columns online in fly-over states, blast me as a femi-Nazi. Can't please everyone.

Still, hard-core leftists enjoy more than enough manpower to rip Coulter, as they routinely do Fox TV host Bill O'Reilly, a man for whom I have the utmost admiration. But this book does not concentrate on pundits who make their living by opinion, but rather on the politicians and starlets who probably should not.

Therefore, you'll find no discussion of Rush Limbaugh, an influential individual whose very existence seems to agitate the left to the point of distraction. He'll have his demons picked over by those who take great glee in conservatives' foibles.

Have at it, folks!

ACKNOWLEDGMENTS

☆

I'D LIKE TO THANK ALL THE PEOPLE who helped me understand the dangers and stupidities of the celebutard set currently infesting Hollywood, Washington and, tragically, New York.

To the two great loves of my life, my gorgeous husband, Mark Phillips, and my beautiful, liberal daughter, Eliza Rose Phillips. You make each day worthwhile.

To my mother, Ruth Peyser, thanks for grounding me and bouncing off ideas every time I hit the wall.

To my editor at Kensington Books, Gary Goldstein, thanks for shaping this book in ways I could not even imagine.

And thanks to the brilliant editors at the *New York Post*, who have always discouraged me from going soft.

Editor in chief Col Allan. Managing editor Jesse Angelo. Publisher Paul Carlucci.

Metropolitan editor Michelle Gotthelf. Assignment editor Dan Greenfield. Photo editor David Boyle. Steve Cuozzo. You guys rock.

To my oldest and best friend, Laura Kilroy.

And to my readers and even critics who, hopefully, will nod their heads in recognition and think, "Who *are* these people?"

CELEBUTARDS

☆

INTRODUCTION

☆

What *Is* a Celebutard?

ce – leb – u – tard (suh – LEB – yu – tard) *noun* **1.** A famous person with a grandiose notion of his own importance and contribution to the known universe. **2.** A human being of sub-par intellect, oversized ego and colossal bank account, whose existence represents a drag on the food chain, waste of oxygen and severe annoyance. **3.** An egregious moron. (Origin: from the Latin *celebutardus Paris Hiltonus maximum Baldwinus*)

> *Sacrificing American soldiers or innocent civilians in an unprecedented pre-emptive attack on a separate, sovereign nation may well prove itself a most temporary medicine.*
> —Sean Penn ad in the *Washington Post*, October 18, 2002

> *I think life's an irrational obsession.*
> —Sean Penn in *Entertainment Weekly*, August 8, 1997

CELEBUTARDS. THEY WALK AMONG US but they are not of us. They eat, sleep and breed just like ordinary humans. But at some magic moment—between the time, say, a movie script wanders into the hands of a world-class celebutard such as George Clooney, and the words travel through lilting vocal chords to land on unsuspect-

1

ing ears, something terrible occurs. They start to believe in their own ignorance.

A dull thinker such as Madonna becomes, in her mind and in the eyes of devoted fans, a self-appointed sage. Veritable moron Rosie O'Donnell transforms from a shrill, gay mom into a rocket scientist. Sean Penn boldly breaks bread with tyrants and enemies of his own country, vapid pop singer Sheryl Crow calls for rationing toilet paper to one sheet per sitting, and earth avenger Al Gore forgets he lost an election. Give a celebutard a microphone and a little encouragement, and suddenly, without warning, that talented performer says and does things that are really, incredibly, grotesquely dumb.

The term celebutard is believed to have first appeared in the *New York Post's* Page Six gossip column, as a compound of celebrity, debutante, and retard. The word is not meant to denigrate those struggling either with youth or with genuine mental challenges. On the contrary, it is a term of art used to describe lazy and egotistical thinkers, stars equipped with abundant money, fame, idle hours and yes-men, who feel secure enough in their own influence and intelligence to create insane foreign or domestic policy in their spare time. It is a choice, rather than an affliction.

In an age in which fabulousness is too often mistaken for gravitas, we must be vigilant. We must know the difference between philosophers and blowhards, between Soren Kierkegaard and Susan Sarandon. We must know our celebutards.

In this book, you will find subjects familiar to readers of my column in the *New York Post* (Hillary, Paris), and also those who've lately leaped onto the national radar by demonstrating an allergic reaction to ordinary moral sense (Laurie David, the mansion-dwelling, SUV hating, ex-wife of Larry).

Now, ladies and gentlemen, we have a winner! At no time since the creation of the celebustocracy has the condition been more evident, more frightening, or more psychically painful than in the case of that grandiose mental midget, the reigning King of the Celebutards, the actor Sean Penn.

1

The Penn Isn't Mightier
Than the Sword

SEAN PENN

☆

THE BROODING, TOUSLE-HAIRED ACTOR, with a style sometimes compared to the late James Dean, was born Sean Justin Penn in Santa Monica, California, on August 17, 1960, the son of director Leo Penn, who was blacklisted during the Communist purge of Hollywood in the 1950s, and actress Eileen Ryan. Though from a young age he had all the makings of a first-class pain-in-the-ass, the young Sean studied not politics, but auto mechanics and speech, when he briefly attended Santa Monica College, soon dropping out. With those sterling credentials, the stage was set for Penn's meteoric rise into celeburoyalty.

Long before he won the best actor Oscar for *Mystic River*, Penn was cast as a world-famous husband, marrying pop singer Madonna in 1985, herself a fledgling member of the celebutard upper crust. Penn quickly distinguished himself on his wedding day by scrawling "F*CK OFF" in giant letters on the roof of their home in California to thwart photographers riding aboard helicopters, in whose direction he reputedly fired a gun. In 1987, he was jailed for beating a photographer.

The Seandonna union unraveled in spectacular fashion, which

was later blamed by the Penn camp on the pop matron's desperate quest for world domination. I guess there just wasn't enough room for two extra-large heads in one family. During an argument over breakfast one morning in December 1988, Penn asked Madonna to leave, later telling *Rolling Stone*, "I made a threat that I would literally cut her hair off. She took it quite seriously." He got that right. Madonna took his words so seriously that she called the cops, and told the authorities that Penn possessed guns. A SWAT team promptly descended on the house, but by this time, Penn was gone.

This led to stories that Penn had tied her up or attacked her with a bat. But Penn, who was charged with felony domestic assault, pleaded guilty to a misdemeanor. The couple divorced in 1989, and have spoken nary a discouraging word about the disastrous union since. Clearly, anger-management sessions with an experienced therapist might have benefited Penn greatly. But he took another path.

Some consumers of popular political culture have traced the birth of Penn's monolithic celebutardistry to his father's refusal to cooperate with the House Un-American Activities Committee, and subsequent descent into working in television, all of which occurred before his son's birth. Actually, the elder Penn may have set the tone in the Penn household, but for at least his early years, the budding actor seemed destined for the pampered, cranky, self-absorbed life of a Hollywood twit.

If only he'd stopped there.

AFTER DECADES of navel-gazing, violent outbursts and method acting, Penn's political idiocy exploded, in all its mind-numbing lunacy, some time after he settled into middle-aged domesticity with actress Robin Wright Penn, with whom he had two children, both born well before they wed in 1996. The couple announced their separation, Hollywood style, to *People* magazine in December 2007, capping an eleven year marriage that equals centuries in celebrity years. But the Penns turned around months later and reconciled,

Penn inartfully dumping the model/professional tsunami survivor Pera Nemcova in the process. Ah—true love!

IN OCTOBER 2002 Penn took out a barely coherent, $56,000 ad in the *Washington Post* that accused President George W. Bush of threatening civil liberties in America and manipulating the media in a rush to war with Iraq.

"I beg you, help save America before yours is a legacy of shame and horror," Penn wrote. And, "Sacrificing American soldiers or innocent civilians in an unprecedented pre-emptive attack on a separate sovereign nation may well prove itself a most temporary medicine."

Hanoi Sean was off and running! Jumping with both feet aboard the anti-war bandwagon, already so popular with the cult of celebutardom, Penn upped the ante by not only glorifying the regime of Saddam Hussein, but failing to make any mention of the atrocities committed by his new best friend. Had he not a hint of shame or conscience? Apparently not, because in December 2002 Penn took a three-day tour of Baghdad, where he met with government officials such as bloodthirsty henchman Tariq Aziz, and was photographed in front of giant posters depicting Saddam. With his matching moustache, sunglasses, cigarette and scowl, Penn bore an alarming resemblance to the Iraqi dictator.

At a press conference, he said, "I feel, both as an American and as a human being, the obligation to accept some level of personal accountability for the policies of my government, both those I support and any that I may not. Simply put, if there is a war or continued sanctions against Iraq, the blood of Americans and Iraqis alike will be on our hands."

However, a month later Penn seemed to have a change of heart. He confessed to Larry King that Saddam had used him as a propaganda tool.

One would think this might spell the end of Penn's free lance diplomacy. It was not to be. A year later, in January 2003, Penn was back in Iraq, to check out the nation, post–American invasion. This time he came as a dilettante journalist, with credentials supplied by *San Francisco Chronicle* editor Phil Bronstein, famed for once having been married to actress Sharon Stone, and for nearly having his toe gnawed off by a Komodo dragon that his then-wife unwisely arranged for him to play with at the Los Angeles Zoo.

In his long and windy dispatches from Iraq published by the *Chronicle* upon his return, Penn bemoans the country's occupation, even while he thanks the troops for saving his behind. "As we race through Fallujah, I take selfish comfort in the sight of black smoke billowing in the aftermath of the recent shelling of a one-story building several hundred yards off the highway, figuring that the closest guerilla fighters might currently be occupied or on the run from U.S. soldiers." So now, the hated soldiers were Penn's saviors.

Finding an offensive act committed by Sean Penn is like finding an orgasm at a Hollywood orgy. There are so many, and some aren't even fake. In August 2005 he flew to that other spoke in the axis of evil, Iran. Attending a Friday night prayer service, Penn heard 10,000 people shouting, in unison, "Death to Israel!" and "Death to America!" Did he finally get the fact that they hate us?

> *Finding an offensive act committed by Sean Penn is like finding an orgasm at a Hollywood orgy.*

"It has always been clear from the Iranian point of view that the call is related to American foreign policy and does not intend to target American people," he wrote in the *Chronicle*. "Many do not subscribe to a literal interpretation of the call for "Death to Israel" and "Death to America."

He did not stop there. "Where had Iran's traumatic experience with American power begun?" Like a rape victim who blamed herself for being attacked, Penn blamed America for the disturbing display.

Some of his antics resulted in slapstick, such as the time Penn turned his sights on saving his own country. In an effort to show up the administration for not doing enough for victims of Hurricane Katrina, Penn, in a white flak jacket and surrounded by a large entourage that included his personal photographer, hopped into a boat on the flooded New Orleans streets, and sailed to the rescue. Or not.

Arriving late into the disaster, Penn evidently forgot to plug a hole in the boat's bottom. In seconds, the vessel filled with water, reported the *Herald-Sun* of Melbourne, Australia. This led the actor to grab a red, plastic cup and frantically bail. Then, the craft's motor failed to start, forcing the occupants to swat the water with paddles. Seeing the boat loaded with cronies and equipment, one bystander taunted, "How are you going to get any people in that thing?"

This near-debacle was followed by a photograph that showed Penn patrolling New Orleans, carrying a shotgun. It wasn't his!, his flack insisted, not quite able to explain why Sean felt the need to pick up a random gun. Some rescuees were nonetheless excited to be saved by a bona fide Hollywood star.

"Guess who come and got me out of the house?" Johnnie Brown, age seventy-three, said over the phone to his sister. "Sean Penn, the actor! The boys were really nice." Later, Penn was furious that his rescue efforts were widely ridiculed as a publicity stunt.

Penn beat out a crowded field competing for the celebutard crown in August 2007, when he visited Venezuelan President Hugo Chavez. The like-minded monster called President Bush "the devil" on the floor of the United Nations a year before, and suggested moving the United Nations to Jerusalem. On Christmas Eve 2006, Chavez angered Jews all over the world when he said, "Some minorities, descendants of the same ones who crucified Christ took all the world's wealth for themselves." This must have thrilled Penn's Jewish family on his father's side.

Penn beat out a crowded field competing for the celebutard crown in August 2007, when he visited Venezuelan President Hugo Chavez.

Chavez courted Penn, praising him for his open letter to the White House, in which he described Bush, Vice President Dick Cheney and Secretary of State Condoleezza Rice as "criminally obscene people."

"I found him a very fascinating guy," Penn told David Letterman. "He's done incredible things for the 80 percent of the people who are poor there." Not a word about Venezuela's human rights abuses. Or Chavez's squelching the freedom of the press. In fact, Penn excused the shutting down of a TV station, saying it had called for Chavez's assassination "so he just did not re-up their license."

I began wondering if Sean Penn, who has the means and stupidity to cavort with tyrants bent on destroying this country, could be tried for treason. But I learned that a charge of treason, while a tantalizing notion, is not an option, since we are not presently at war with Venezuela or Iran and Saddam Hussein is long gone. Besides, this country, with all its warts, is far more tolerant of those who rail against it, and quite a bit more protective of those who would do it harm, than any of the tin pot dictators that Penn so admires.

The only recourse the public has against this captain of the celebutards is simply to refuse to see his films.

2

An Inconvenient Goof

AL GORE

During my service in the United States Congress I took the initiative in creating the Internet. I took the initiative in moving forward a whole range of initiatives that have proven to be important to our county's economic growth and environmental protection, improvements to our education system.

—Al Gore on CNN, 1999

AT FIRST BLUSH, it may appear problematic to include a meditation on the wit and idiocy of Al Gore in a book that also includes a chapter dedicated to Paris Hilton. Gore, after all, served time in the House of Representatives, the United States Senate and as vice president to the Clinton White House. Paris served time.

Gore presided over a panel dedicated to cutting government waste and mismanagement. Paris presided over the Bimbo Summit, populated by vice maniacs Britney Spears and Lindsay Lohan. She is also blond.

Still, I would argue that Al and Paris have far more in common than is readily apparent at first examination. Both have won fame, fortune and the best possible restaurant tables due to their fawning entrée into that most American of institutions, Hollywood. Both

9

have drawn attention to themselves, while laying claim to world-wide importance, influence, and privilege, while developing an A-list following of think-alike lemmings. Only Gore starred in an Oscar-winning movie, and has an Emmy and a Nobel Peace Prize sitting on his mantle. But Paris is still young.

Albert Arnold Gore Jr. was born March 31, 1948, in Washington, D.C., to his namesake father, then a United States representative who would later serve in the Senate, and Pauline LaFon Gore. He split his childhood between Washington and Carthage, Tennessee. With a relatively high IQ (it's been gauged at between 133 and 134) he quickly grew bored at Harvard and scored at the lower end of his class, before discovering a passion for his father's business—politics. Switching majors from English to government, he graduated with honors.

Then Gore joined the Army. He served during the Vietnam era, and was shipped to Southeast Asia for about five months, though he has always maintained his vehement opposition to the conflict. After his discharge, he worked for five years as a reporter for the *Nashville Tennessean* for what he called "slightly above slave wages"—though he also benefited handsomely from royalties paid by owners of zinc mines that operated on his family's Tennessee farm. One thing was certain: Gore would not languish long in journalistic obscurity.

In 1970, he married Mary Elizabeth Aitcheson, known as Tipper. She would flirt solo with her own celebutardom by pushing in the 1980s for parental warnings on records containing dirty lyrics, and also through her self-serving announcement, during the run-up to the 2000 presidential election, that she had gone through a teensy weensy "situational depression"—but got all better.

Gore was enrolled in law school at Vanderbilt University in 1976 when he quit to run for a seat in the House of Representatives. He won. And thus, a political career was born, one that would occupy his days for more than two decades, until it was abruptly cut short by a crushing defeat that sent Gore into a tailspin of disappointment and self-pity. And put him on a quest to, once again, feel relevant.

But first, Gore's life took another turn. On April 3, 1989, his six-year-old son, Albert, was nearly killed in a car crash while leaving the Baltimore Orioles' opening day game. As Little Albert convalesced, Big Albert started writing his book, *Earth in the Balance,* about environmental conservation. This tome became the first book written by a Senator to make The *New York Times* best seller list since John F. Kennedy's *Profiles in Courage.* It also provided Al Gore with a nifty subject around which to build his second act.

How different Gore's life would have turned out were it not for a close election, the Sunshine State, and a president named Bush. How different for us all.

The 2000 race was said to be Gore's to lose, and he did lose it, in wild fashion. The election pitted the popular Gore against the popular Texas Governor George W. Bush. But Gore miscalculated when he declined to procure the advice, counsel and star wattage of Bill Clinton, who remained wildly popular in spite of—or because of—his Oval Office affair with an intern named Monica Lewinsky. Gore thought he was better off going it alone than

Gore would never again so badly underestimate the intelligence of the American people.

saddled with his undisciplined former boss. Gore would never again so badly underestimate the intelligence of the American people.

If the 2000 vote was close on a national level, in Florida, as Dan Rather would say in the throes of election night aneurysm: "This race is tight like a too-small bathing suit on a too-long ride home from the beach." Election Day came and went, with no clear winner in Florida. Hanging in the balance were the state's twenty-five electoral votes, without which a candidate could not take the whole enchilada. The country waited.

Hand recounts were ordered in a few heavily Democratic counties in the southeastern part of the state. Poll workers examined individual ballots under magnifying glasses, trying to divine "voter intent." And so, we all learned more than we ever needed to know about chads—those tiny bits of paper that are punched out of paper ballots. We learned about hanging chads (nibs that are incompletely punched out of ballots) and pregnant ones (chads that are pushed in the middle, but not torn out). Evidently, Florida stands alone on the planet as the place where one may be a little bit pregnant.

The election was finally decided by the United States Supreme Court, which ended the legal bickering and allowed Florida, finally, to certify its vote. Bush won the state by just 534 votes, out of 5.8 million cast, barely enough to take a high school election. On January 20, 2001, George W. Bush was sworn in as the 43rd president of the United States. He was only the fourth man in history to lose the popular vote—by more than a half million—but win the Electoral College, and therefore the election.

But his victory would be cemented four years later. In 2004, with the Florida fiasco still fresh in voters' minds, more than 55 percent of the American electorate turned out to vote, compared with just over 51 percent in 2000. This time, Bush won a decisive majority over Democrat John Kerry. The voters had spoken, but the Democrats didn't really want to hear.

The stinging 2000 loss hit Gore hard. For the first time in his adult life, he was out of a job. He would make up for it by transcending politics and appealing to his natural celebrity base to grasp more fame and power than he might have received had he been elected president.

When he was vice president, Gore was in charge of "Reinventing Government." This brought him a spot on *The Late Show With David Letterman* in 1993, in which Gore, who'd unearthed federal regulations for smashing an ashtray—it "should break into a small number of irregular shaped pieces, not greater in number than 35"—tried to break an ashtray according to government code. Gore had a reputation for being a stuffed shirt, but he clearly reveled in the *Late Show* applause. Still, there exists little star power in ashtrays, or in Gore's dubious claim to having brought about the digital age. To succeed in this game, Al Gore would reach higher.

And he did. Gore emerged into the public consciousness in spectacular fashion in 2006, starring in the global warming documentary *An Inconvenient Truth*—a glitzy manifesto about the dangers of climate change. It had all the drama and pacing of a Hollywood horror flick, capable of scaring the bejeezus out of small children and senior citizens. It also promoted a view of global warming that was deeply, alarmingly, and exploitatively flawed.

But facts held little sway to burgeoning legions of Gore disciples, to whom the warming of the planet was not a matter of science, nor of politics, but something akin to religion.

"My fellow Americans, people all over the world," Gore said onstage at the Kodak Theater in Hollywood, in February 2007, as *An Inconvenient Truth* won the Academy Award for Best Documentary Feature. "We need to solve the climate crisis. It's not a political issue; it's a moral issue. We have everything we need to get started, with the possible exception of the will to act."

Apparently one should do as Gore says, not as he does. While Gore was sermonizing about energy conservation, his Nashville estate was drinking electricity and natural gas at a rate of twenty times the national average— burning through nearly 221,000 kilowatt hours per year, compared to a national average of 10,656, according to Nashville Electric Service records unearthed by the Tennessee Center for Policy Reseacrch.

> *While Gore was sermonizing about energy conservation, his Nashville estate was drinking electricity and natural gas at a rate of 20 times the national average.*

An Inconvenient Truth is jampacked with the type of Tinseltown fear-mongering capable of keeping one awake at night—huge increases in sea levels, melting ice sheets, rampant tropical diseases, and hurricanes that make the twister in *The Wizard of Oz* look like a gentle breeze. I have no interest in venturing an opinion here as to whether climate change actually exists, but rather to throw a little cold water on some of Gore's most outlandish claims.

First, it is fact, inconvenient as it may be, that the Arctic was as warm or warmer than it is today in 1940. Further, there is evidence that the Greenland ice sheet is actually growing. As Massachusetts Institute of Technology professor of atmospheric sciences Richard S. Lindzen wrote in the *Wall Street Journal*, many glaciers stopped retreating in about 1970, and some are now advancing again. And, while hurricanes have been blamed on global warming by the Gore crowd, scientists won't attribute any particular hurricane to the change in climate.

Yes, Dr. Lindzen agrees, the planet is warmer. The scientific community has pretty much agreed since 1988 that the earth is one degree Fahrenheit hotter than it was a century ago. But temperatures have remained flat since 1998. And those greenhouse gases? No question they've increased in the atmosphere. But their impact on warming is theoretical, and scientists are left scratching their heads as to why the world isn't warmer than it is.

Furthermore, Gore disciples are passionate that global cooking is a distinctly American problem, solvable only by the United States making sacrifices that polluted bastions like China, whose coal-fired ovens spew filth into the heavens, should not be required to make. Never discussed are the gains in economics, education and standard of living made by developing nations that adopt modern technology, and therefore increase pollution. And don't expect Al Gore to stop jetting across the globe to make speeches and retrieve prizes. Some sacrifices, I suppose, are too great to expect.

Gore picked up an Emmy award for the interactive cable and satellite channel he launched aimed at youth, Current TV, as well as for his work on global warming. Yes, 2007 was shaping up as a very good year.

But perhaps the biggest blow to Gore's fantasies of being elected global savior was dealt by a British judge in October 2007. A father had requested that High Court Judge Michael Burton pull Gore's movie from schools because it contained, as the dad put it, "serious scientific inaccuracies, political propaganda and sentimental mush." Judge Burton refused to ban the film outright, but he decreed that the movie should only be shown in British schools along with guidance notes to prevent political indoctrination.

The judge determined that the film contained nine fatal errors. They are:

Error No. 1: Gore asserted that a sea-level rise of up to 20 feet would be caused by melting of ice sheets "in the near future."

Judge's response: "This [is] distinctly alarmist" and will only occur "after, and over, millennia."

Error No. 2: Low-lying Pacific atolls have already been evacuated.

Judge: There is no evidence of an evacuation having happened.

Error No. 3: The Gulf Stream, which warms up the Atlantic Ocean, would shut down.

Judge: It was "very unlikely" it would shut down in the future, though it might slow down.

Error No. 4: Graphs showing a rise in CO_2 and the rise in temperature over a period of 650,000 years showed "an exact fit."

Judge: A connection exists, but "the two graphs do not establish what Mr. Gore asserts."

Error No. 5: The disappearance of snow on Mount Kilimanjaro is due to global warming.

Judge: It cannot be established that the recession of snows on Mount Kilimanjaro is mainly attributable to human-induced climate change.

Error No. 6: The drying up of Lake Chad is a prime example of a catastrophic result of global warming.
Judge: Insufficient evidence exists to establish the exact cause.

Error No. 7: Hurricane Katrina was caused by global warming.
Judge: There is "insufficient evidence to show that."

Error No. 8: This one is my personal favorite: Gore claimed polar bears were being found that had drowned "swimming long distances—up to 60 miles—to find the ice."
Judge: Only four bears have been found drowned, and because of a storm.

Error No. 9: Coral reefs were bleaching because of global warming and other factors.
Judge: Separating the impact of stresses due to climate change from other stresses faced by the reefs, such as over-fishing and pollution, was difficult.

This ruling, however, failed to prevent the brain trust in Oslo from awarding Gore and the United Nations Intergovernmental Panel on Climate Change the 2007 Nobel Peace Prize—a prestigious award that in recent years went to President Jimmy Carter, as well as Palestine Liberation Organization chairman, thief to his people, and terrorist leader, Yasser Arafat.

Splitting the prize between Gore and the UN panel struck some as odd because the two institutions do not see eye-to-eye on climate change.

The UN panel, Gore's co-winner, predicts a sea level rise of 13 inches by the years 2100. In *An Inconvenient Truth*, as well as a Gore-authored book by the same name, "he showed an undated montage of Florida sliding beneath the waves"—representing a sea rise of 13 feet or more, wrote Patrick J. Michaels, senior fellow for environmental studies at the Cato Institute, who counts himself a member of the UN Intergovernmental Panel on Climate Change.

Michaels also pointed out a truth Gore might find—here we go again—not terribly convenient: computer models mentioned by the UN show Antarctica actually gaining ice this century, because slight warming will result in more precipitation, which will fall as snow.

Gore's stock answer to his various naysayers and detractors, both laymen and those employed by the scientific community, is as smug as it is insulting: He heckles them. The true Gore was exposed while he was out campaigning with congressional candidates in Seattle in 2006. Gore was told about the views of Republican Representative Dave Reichert, who politely expressed doubts about the gospel of global warming. Gore cracked, "You know, 15 percent of people believe the moon landing was staged on some movie lot and a somewhat smaller number still believe the Earth is flat. They get together on Saturday night and party with the global-warming deniers."

Global warming. It's more than science. Or politics. Or even religion.

It's a cult, and Al Gore is the man passing out the Kool-Aid. Heaven help the human who dares disagree.

3

Patron Saint of Stupidity
BARBRA STREISAND

He's very intelligent, very, very sensitive, very evolved; more than his linear years. And he's an extraordinary human being. He plays like a Zen master. It's very in the moment.

> —Barbra Streisand, then fifty, on twenty-two-year-old tennis player Andre Agassi, 1992 U.S. Open

Shut the f@$! up, would you? Shut up if you can't take a joke.

> —Barbra dresses down a heckler, Madison Square Garden, October 2006

The arrogance of this C student who maligns his opponents' crediblity by calling them flip floppers, is the biggest flip flopper himself! When debating Al Gore during the 2000 presidential elections, Bush spoke against nation building, yet went into Iraq a year later to national build . . . which we now see has resulted in disaster.

> —Barbra vs. President George W. Bush on her Web site, March 2006

IN THE CROWDED CELEBUTARD FIELD, there exists stiff competition for the title of Dumbest Woman Alive. Let's take a look . . .

Nancy Pelosi tries to grant a tax break to Venezuelan dictator Hugo Chavez. Madonna catches a phony British accent. Sheryl Crow campaigns for a limit of one sheet of toilet paper per flush. And Lindsay Lohan and Britney Spears prove that literacy (nor panties) are not necessary assets for young ladies. Yet for all the sheer idiocy commonly displayed by starlets and politicians today, it is the elder stateswoman of bimbos who wins the prize, daily demonstrating that a brain is an optional accessory provided a lady has money, fame and adoring fans.

The planet's dumbest woman has been famous longer than the younger generation has breathed, yet she shows, time and again, a breathtaking lack of awareness of her own mental shortcomings.

On her personal Web site, we see the unfiltered rantings of this unglued diva. In speeches and in stage appearances, which patrons pay big bucks to endure, we get to know a lady so fundamentally dim, she should be placed under glass and studied. Yet there she goes again and again, proving that passable grammar and common self-knowledge are commodities as rare as gifted singing pipes. She is Barbra Streisand. She is our patron saint of stupidity.

When did she begin to go off the rails?

She was born Barbara Joan Streisand (yes, her name originally was spelled the ordinary way) on April 24, 1942, in Brooklyn, New York, to Emanuel Streisand, a grammar school teacher who died when she was just fifteen-months old, and Diana, a school secretary. Her mother discouraged young Barbara from going into show business because she did not think her little girl was pretty enough to cut it, and suggested that she learn to type instead. Where have I heard this story before? Right. It sounds like a treatment for the 1968 movie *Funny Girl*. In it, Barbra, as she came to be known, starred as a plain but talented, Jewish gal (it's based on the life of showgirl Fanny Brice) with skinny legs and a big nose who transforms into a swan after she falls in love with wicked Nicky Arnstein, played by a swarthy Omar Sharif. It's a pretty fantasy, for which Barbra, appearing in her first movie, split a best actress Oscar with Katharine Hepburn.

In real life, Barbara dropped the second "A" in her first name shortly after moving to Manhattan after graduating from high school. She was unconventional-looking enough, with a powerful enough singing voice, to pull off the transformation from ugly duckling to American beauty. Despite her mother's nagging, she never attended a day of college. Why should she? Barbra Streisand learned from an early age never to let her natural deficiencies hold her back.

Barbra is a singer, that much is not in dispute except, perhaps, in her own brain. She started singing professionally in a gay bar and quickly signed a record deal. Along the way she has won Emmys, Grammys and a pair of Academy Awards—one for acting, the other for Best Song—and became one of the top selling female solo acts of all time, before coming full circle and tying Liza Minnelli as the most popular diva parodied in gay karaoke bars. But Barbra didn't want to be known as a singer. She badly wanted to be an actress, and therein lies the tension. She did have success on Broadway and in the movies, starting with *Funny Girl*, but it was her voice the people tuned in to. Eventually, she started producing and directing her own films, including the horrifically embarrassing 1983 movie *Yentl*, in which Barbra at age forty-one, plays a teenage yeshiva student. Eight years later she put out *Prince of Tides*, a romance in which her self-conscious and immobile face, trained to tilt toward its good side, appears as if it's filmed through gauze. Mercifully, she refrained from making films for a while after that.

Streisand married actor Elliot Gould in 1963, shortly before turning twenty-one, and divorced him eight years later. The union produced a son, Jason. The list of men she is said to have dated is long and varied, from Ryan O'Neal, Tom Smothers, Warren Beatty (who hasn't?), to Jon Voight, Canadian Prime Minister Pierre Trudeau, producer Jon Peters, Omar Sharif, Don Johnson, Steve McQueen, Kris Kristofferson, Peter Jennings and, at age fifty, a twenty-two year-old Andre Agassi. That pairing evidently could not survive the day an out-to-lunch Barbra gushed about her "Zen master" on live TV during the 1992 U.S. Tennis Open in New York. In 1998, twenty-seven years after divorcing Elliot Gould, she walked down the aisle with James Brolin, a quiet (compared to Barbra) actor who in recent years appeared on TV in commercials as the Midas man.

I have to conclude that Streisand feels unfulfilled by a career that made her an international superstar, worth an estimated $300 million. She wanted to be an actress. Instead, she's settled on being a singer who sometimes acts, moving into mature (thank God), charicaturish roles such as that of Roz Focker in 2004's *Meet the Fockers* with Dustin Hoffman. At least she kept on her shirt. (She took it off, to her regret and that of millions of movie-goers, in 1970's *The Owl and the Pussycat*.)

Streisand raised a ton of cash for Bill Clinton before the 1992 presidential election, and performed at his inaugural gala. In fact, Barbra has raised more money for Democrats than just about any celebutard worth his Screen Actors Guild card. This has given her permission to produce a personal Web site in which she's made a slew of horrifying goofs that would cause a woman with an ordinary sense of shame to blush crimson. But we're talking about Barbra here.

Her site is a spellbinding mix of giant ego and complete lack of an internal mirror. It features dozens of soft-focus pictures of the star trying to look serious. The purpose of the thing seems to be to give the public, clamoring for all things Barbra, insight into a mish mash of her political views, as well as piquish responses to tabloid reports (which she calls Truth Alerts). And in case you still haven't realized whom this site is about, her press releases, including one in which she endorses Hillary Clinton for president, include this helpful description: "Legendary filmmaker, artist, and Democratic activist Barbra Streisand." No wonder the makers of *Comedy Central*'s show *South Park* routinely prod her like a pinata. She's too easy.

On September 25, 2002, Streisand, along with her "political

consultant" Margery Tabankin, faxed a memo to House Minority Leader Dick Gephardt, urging "Democrats to get off the defensive and go on the offensive" against Republicans and the war on terror. The problem is, the memo was addressed to Dick "Gebhart," a laugh riot first reported on the DrudgeReport. Also misspelled in the memo is Saddam Hussein—as "Sadam," and al-Qaeda as "Al Queda." Worse, on her Web site, Barbra admitted a tiny goof—the memo was faxed initially not to a Democratic politician such as Gephardt (Gebhart to Babs), but to the office of a Republican. (Tabankin used the classic chick excuse: She said she and Barbra were "emotional" during the faxing.)

La Streisand handled her gaffe the time-tested celebutard way: She blamed an underling. In a Truth Alert, Barbra explained that she dictated her memo over the phone to a new staffer. "THE IRONIC FURTHER TRUTH," the alert continued—a posting evidently not dictated to a staffer but posted by the illiterate diva herself— "Hidden in this example of diverted news priorities is the fact that Barbra Streisand is a great speller, meticulous in her written communications!"

She continued, "The incident illustrates how the Democratic message concerning the failures of this Republican administration are repeatedly pushed aside in the media, pre-empted by silly side-issues. The real truth, the really important and relevant truth" (as opposed to the really unimportant and not terribly significant truth) "is having a hard time getting through."

Days later, an unbowed Babs was onstage at a National Democratic Gala in Hollywood when she opened her yap, and thus made herself into an even bigger fool.

"I find George Bush and Cheney frightening," Streisand said. "Donald Rumsfeld and John Ashcroft frightening . . . I find bringing the country to the brink of war unilaterally five weeks before an election questionable—and very, very frightening . . ." Good, Barbra. You've studied the names of cabinet members.

But then, she said, "You know, really good artists have a way of being relevant in their time . . . but great artists are relevant at any-time. So, in the words of William Shakespeare, 'Beware the leader who bangs the drums of war in order to whip the citizenry into a patriotic fervor, for patriotism is indeed a double-edged sword. It both emboldens the blood, just as it narrows the mind . . . And when the drums of war have reached a fever pitch and the blood boils with hate and the mind has closed, the leader will have no need in seizing the rights of the citizenry. Rather, the citizenry, in-fused with fear and blinded with patriotism, will offer up all of their rights unto the leader, and gladly so. How do I know? For this is what I have done. And I am Caesar.'"

She continued, "Imagine that was written over 400 years ago . . . It's amazing how history without consciousness is destined to re-peat itself. So . . . from the words of William Shakespeare to the words of Irving Berlin . . ."

Guess what, literature fans? Shakespeare never wrote those words. In fact, the first time these lines appeared anywhere was on the Internet, in the form of mass e-mails. Streisand, it would ap-pear, had fallen for a hoax. A hoax it would have taken a ten-year-old five minutes to uncover!

Would the diva admit to a mistake? You might as well ask Bar-bra Streisand to undo her nose job.

"The authorship of this is important," she wrote defensively on her site, "but it doesn't detract from the fact that the words them-selves are powerful and true and beautifully written. Whoever wrote this is talented and should be writing their own play." Wait a minute—so Barbra is using the Dan Rather defense, which the ex-CBS anchor perfected when caught reporting on fake military memos. She's saying that the truth doesn't really matter at all, as long as you like what you're reporting. Maybe she should relaunch her Truth Alerts as BS Alerts.

You say "Iraqi." I say "Iranian." Heck, if you're one of the biggest-selling female artists of all time, I guess you can call the late Saddam Hussein the leader of Israel if it suits you. Weeks after the Shakespeare debacle, Barbra was again at the top of her ignoramus game, posting a Truth Alert entitled, "REPUBLICAN CONGRESSIONAL CANDIDATE ATTACKS BARBRA STREISAND IN ADS IN DESPERATE EFFORT TO CUT INTO CAROLYN McCARTHY LEAD."

Writing in the third person, Barbra complained about an ad run by congressional candidate Marilyn O'Grady, who accused her—Barbra says unfairly—of defending Saddam Hussein. O'Grady ran against New York Democratic Representative Carolyn McCarthy, a noted champion for gun control.

Her alert said: "A Republican/Conservative candidate trying with fading hopes to unseat respected Democratic Congresswoman Carolyn McCarthy made a last-ditch effort to win headlines by devising ads in which she blatantly misquoted Barbra Streisand, fabricating outrageous quotes and completely misrepresenting Ms. Streisand's deep opposition to the Iranian dictator, Saddam Hussein . . ."

Huh?

Streisand's response was typically obfuscating. And offensive. "This is another example of the Republican way of trying to discredit the messenger before the public can get the message. Ms. O'Grady's deceitful radio and tv ads put egregiously fabricated words in Ms. Streisand's mouth. . . ."

At least she didn't blame anyone else. Her Web site, incidentally, finally located the country of Saddam's origin and corrected it. It's Iraq, Barbra. Not Iran. Not Iraque . . .

But this was all topped with a big, red bow by a posting she threw up (pun intended) on her site in March 2006. The post is long. It's loopy. It's a wonder Streisand hit "Send" before tossing it through the spellchecker. I will cut to the chase, and start with the fourth sentence. All misspellings are the author's:

"In the 1970's, during the Nixon Adminstration, serious political curruption arose and the Republican leadership stepped up and took responsibilty by holding hearings and subpoening administration officials." Four spelling errors—in one sentence!

"Eventually, the President was forced to resign rather than face impeachment preceedings that likely would have been successful."

Oh, it goes on. And on. Streisand feebly tries to make a point about administration accountability. Or something. (Should I say sumthing?)

"It is clear that today's Republican Congressional leaders are not prepared to hold this President accountable. Therefore, it's critical that people elect members of the Democratic party to the House and Senate so that a new leadership can take control. Only if this occurs, can we even begin to imagine a time when there will be a myriad of investigations so desperately needed on so many issues . . . let alone the ultimate investigation which would involve the conduct of the President of the United States and the determination of whether his actions warrented impeachment proceedings."

"The arrogance of this C student who maligns his opponents' crediblity by calling them flip floppers, is the biggest flip flopper himself! When debating Al Gore during the 2000 presidential elections, Bush spoke against nation building, yet went into Irag a year later to national build . . . which we now see has resulted in disaster."

It is almost too much to bear. Aside from the hideously ungrammatical sentence that leads the previous paragraph, and in addition to the obvious misspelling of "Iraq," she asserts that the United States invaded the country in 2001. Even a D student knows that happened in 2003. But the zaniest aspect of her run-on rant is that the woman who failed to attend a minute of college denigrates Bush as an arrogant "C student." Bush in fact earned a Master's of Business Administration degree at Harvard, after earning his undergraduate degree at Yale. While his grade-point average at Yale was a relatively lackluster 77, it should be noted that John Kerry, Bush's Democratic opponent in the 2004 election, graduated from the same institution two years before Bush, earning an average of just 76.

Here's a complete list of the meticulous one's misspellings:

Irag. Curruption. Dictatoriship. Crediblity. Adminstration (three times). Warrented. Desperatly. Preceedings. Ouside. Subpoening. Responsibilty.

Take some responsibility, Babs! A short time after the posting, Streisand's spokesmouth, Dick Guttman, blamed the errors on the star's Web hosting company.

There was no disputing the identity of the woman at the microphone in New York's Madison Square Garden in October 2006. That's when Streisand, appearing for the first time since a 2000 farewell concert (she always says goodbye, but never leaves) got irritated by a heckler who didn't like her skit involving an impersonator of George W. Bush. Frankly, most of the audience, which included a good number of Bush-bashers grew a tad impatient with the tedious politicization of the concert. One fan yelled out something that sounded like, "Communist!" That's when Streisand blew her stack.

"Shut the f*ck up, would you?" she shouted, slowly and clearly enunciating the third word. "Shut up if you can't take a joke!"

She shrieked, "Give him his money back! Go get your money back!" The man left. I hope she returned every penny.

> Barbra later apologized, but defended her shrewish outburst insanely. "The artist's role is to disturb."

Barbra later apologized, but defended her shrewish outburst insanely. "The artist's role is to disturb."

There is only one thing disturbing about Barbra Streisand. It's that anyone, anywhere, continues to listen to a word that comes out of this gold-throated dolt's mouth.

4

Clooney Tunes

GEORGE CLOONEY

☆

*You can't beat your enemy anymore through wars;
instead you create an entire generation of people
revenge-seeking. These days, it only matters who's in
charge. Right now that's us—for a while at least. Our
opponents are going to resort to car bombs and suicide
attacks because they have no other way to win.*

—George Clooney on German TV, 2003

*Run for office? No. I've slept with too many women, I've
done too many drugs, and I've been to too many parties.*

—Clooney on politics

"No, I'm gay gay. The third gay was pushing it."

—Clooney to *Esquire* magazine in April 2008 responding to a
website claiming he was "gay, gay, gay."

HE'S THE BIGGEST STAR to grace the heavens, envied by men, adored
by women. Heck, adored by men and slobbered over by women.
He's also a major political iconoclast, who cut his $20 million
Ocean's Eleven salary to $1 to star in, co-write, direct and produce

the socially conscious, historically illiterate propaganda picture set in the McCarthy era, *Good Night and Good Luck*.

Probably more than any adult man alive, George Clooney appears on "celebrity lists" popularized by the HBO series *Entourage*. This is when otherwise monogamous couples draw up lists of famous people who the couple agrees that, should the opportunity arise, the woman would be permitted to sleep with, no penalties to the relationship. On *Entourage*, star Adrian Grenier discovers to his dismay that the woman with whom he'd spent the night was about to get married, but had put him on her list—so sex was OK, but just that one time. Of course, if you want to trap Clooney for more than a few hours, you'd better be exceptionally selfless, politically liberal, uncommonly stunning and most of all, patient, because George has a chronic inability to settle down. This tendency was joked upon in New York's Madame Tussaud's Wax Museum, where a sculpture in Clooney's likeness sits at a table offering a faux diamond ring to whoever sits opposite. How many tourists have had their pictures snapped in the fantasy pose of getting engaged to George Clooney?

His CHRONIC SINGLEDOM has also led Clooney to battle persistent rumors that he is swinging for the boys' team. *Esquire* magazine asked him in April 2008 about a Web site that asserts "George Clooney is gay, gay, gay."

"No, I'm gay, gay," George cheerfully said. "The third gay, that was pushing it."

But movie tough guy Clooney went soft when addressing a 2007 shoving match in a Los Angeles restaurant with cover model and "I Can't Believe It's Not Butter" pitch man Fabio. Clooney had asked a member of Fabio's party to refrain from taking his picture. But Fabio insisted he was merely hosting a charity event when a drunken Clooney flipped the bird and insulted Fabio's female guests.

"He has no class," Fabio huffed to *OK* magazine. "You have to be a low-class scumbag to start calling a woman a name. If you're a man, you should never. You should be a gentleman. These women were with me and as a man I defend them. He was lucky he ran out of the restaurant. He's not even half a man."

Clooney agreed the Italian-born model and romance novelist could beat him up.

"Yeah, that's probably true," said Clooney. "He's a big guy."

Before his TV success, Clooney was married from 1989 to 1993 to actress Talia Balsam. More recently he's developed a reputation as a consummate bachelor. Nicole Kidman and Michelle Pfeiffer once bet him $10,000 that he'd have kids by age forty. But when he hit forty-one and still had failed to reproduce, Clooney confessed, Kidman sent him a big check. But the star sent it back, betting double or nothing he'd be childless by age fifty.

And why not? At a glitzy 2007 Hollywood AIDS benefit, Sharon Stone put Clooney on the auction block along with his *Ocean's Thirteen* co-stars Matt Damon, Don Cheadle, Andy Garcia and Ellen Barkin, with the high bidder winning a kiss from the bachelor of his or her choice. Sorry, Matt, Andy, Don and Ellen, there never was any contest. Some bazillionaire bid $350,000 to watch Clooney kiss his girlfriend on the mouth, proving that the "celebrity list" is alive and well. When you're the sexiest mammal alive, kisses don't come cheap or private.

He has held on tightly to his confirmed bachelorhood. Standing next to girlfriend Sarah Larson in New York in 2007, he said, "I'm never at home and every woman gets sick of it. If I was them, I wouldn't put up with me for too long."

BUT IT WAS CLOONEY who didn't put up with Larson for long. After a year of togetherness, he dumped the former cocktail waitress in May 2008, leaving his Los Angeles mansion for a time so Larson, twenty-nine, could gather her stuff. "George is relieved to be single again," a friend of Clooney's reportedly said. "He thinks Sarah is sweet [yee-ouch!] and that is why it is so hard to break up with her." Larson was said to be completely devastated. Clooney had just celebrated his forty-seventh birthday with her. She was his Oscars date. She thought he was about to propose marriage. Instead, those pesky gay rumors returned, full-force.

Twice voted *People* magazine's "Sexiest Man Alive," Clooney is a former TV heartthrob (he catapulted to stardom playing hunky Dr. Doug Ross in *ER*) who clawed his way to the top of the celebrity acting game with his deadpan delivery, full head of hair and air of inaccessibility. But somewhere along the line, Clooney translated his public adulation into an annoying willingness to express whatever offensive or inane liberal patter crosses his graying head.

"I'm going to keep saying 'liberal' as loud as I can and as often as I can," Clooney told *Newsweek* magazine. Somehow, he was talking about his film *Good Night, and Good Luck.*

Clooney does a pretty good impersonation of a guy who doesn't care about dough (he earned a paltry $350,000 and a best-supporting actor Oscar for *Syriana*). But then he rakes in $10 million, $15 million, even $20 million for a mainstream flick that pays for his money-losing political diatribes. As he's risen in prominence, and, unbelievably, influence—some folks have urged him to run for office in his native Kentucky—Clooney has come down with an acute case of Clooney's Disease, a disorder that occurs when actors begin to believe their own hype.

> *Clooney has come down with an acute case of Clooney's Disease, a disorder that occurs when actors begin to believe their own hype. The afflicted are deluded into thinking fame makes them smarter and their opinions more important than those of ordinary mortals.*

The afflicted are deluded into thinking fame makes them smarter and their opinions more important than those of ordinary mortals. In 2003, as Clooney received a special filmmaking achievement award from the National Board of Reviews, he joked, cruelly, "Charleston Heston announced again today that he is suffering from Alzheimer's." Turns out Clooney is active in gun control, but what that has to do with a filmmaking award exists only in his frazzled head. Clooney defended his remark to columnist Liz Smith. "I don't care. Charlton Heston is the head of the National Rifle Association. He deserves what anyone says about him."

Replied Heston, "It just goes to show that sometimes class does skip a generation," referring to Clooney's elegant late aunt, Rosemary Clooney.

Perhaps Clooney thought he was too cute to be an idiot, a theme that crops up repeatedly in his life and work. But George Clooney proved something unintentional with the Heston remark: Good-looking people, even more than Alzheimer's patients, have an inverse ability to be stupendously dumb.

George Timothy Clooney was born May 6, 1961, in Lexington, Kentucky, to Nick Clooney, a journalist, TV anchorman, game show host, host of TV's *American Movie Classics*, and failed Democratic congressional candidate, and Nina Bruce, a former beauty pageant queen. His cousins include actor Miguel Ferrer, the son of Rosemary and Jose Ferrer.

"I spent the first part of my life being referred to as Rosemary Clooney's brother, and now I am spending the last part of my life being referred to as George Clooney's dad," his father famously said, with a touch of bitterness.

Clooney attended Northern Kentucky University and briefly the University of Cincinnati, but did not graduate. I sense a trend— why do those with the silliest, loudest mouths tend to be the least educated? He turned to acting only after he failed a tryout with the Cincinnati Reds.

While still appearing on *ER*, Clooney began starring in feature films. These included 1997's *Batman and Robin*, in which he played the conflicted bat, a role he said he hated. He told Barbara Walters that, in his rubber suit and pert nipples, he also played Batman gay.

It seems Clooney quickly forgot that, as a struggling, young actor living under Aunt Rosemary's roof, he couldn't get arrested to get his picture taken by that breed of photographer known as paparazzi. Or "stalkerazzi," as he called some of the most aggressive shutterbugs. Once a star in 1996, he organized a boycott by fellow celebs of *Entertainment Tonight* because its parent company owned *Hard Copy*, which he considered the worst invader of celebrity privacy.

Clooney objected to photographers (A) yelling comments such as "Who's the fat chick?" about a woman he was with to get his reaction, and (B) shooting over the top of his stall in a men's room, which happened in Australia. In that incident, Clooney grabbed the peeping shooter's film from his camera, which prompted police to begin an investigation into Clooney's alleged photographic assault. But the probe was dropped once cops saw the pictures, which Clooney then destroyed. The episode leaves me wondering what Clooney found so objectionable about the sight of his presumably naked body in the loo.

A year later, Princess Diana was killed, and Clooney, loudly and unfairly, blamed the photographers who chased her into a Paris tunnel. His criticism grew so shrill that those who make their living bringing Clooney fame and fortune had enough of his whining. At the New York premiere of his film, *The Peacemaker*, photographers stood quietly together, put down their cameras, and refused to shoot.

After Diana's death, Steve Coz, editor of the *National Enquirer*, called for all tabloids to boycott "motorcycle paparazzi"—the breed that chases its prey from the backs of bikes. Oddly, despite the unprecedented self-censorship, Clooney singled out Coz for condemnation. "The Princess of Wales is dead, and you [Coz] have gone on television, and you have washed your hands, and you have deflected responsibility, and yet I wonder how you sleep at night. You should be ashamed." Perhaps Clooney failed to actually *read* the loathed tabloids.

But in 2005, Clooney suddenly came out against anti-celebrity stalking laws championed by fellow thespians such as Reese Witherspoon.

"These guys can be real jerks, these paparazzi, they're not trying to catch me doing something stupid, which I'll have to take hits for—they're trying to create you doing something stupid. They walk through the airport and go, 'Who's that fat chick you're with?'

"I'll take all of those hits in lieu of trying to restrict it, because the dangers of restricting it, or getting into those dangers, [is] like burning the first book. I get that they do some rotten things . . . It's a drag for me . . . [But] as a guy who believes in the free press, I think that some of these hits we have to take in order to not mess with freedom of speech."

After Clooney and Sarah Larson were injured in a 2007 motorcycle accident in New Jersey, more than two-dozen hospital staffers were suspended for peeking at his medical records. But Clooney, undergoing a change of heart over invasions of privacy, said they should not be punished.

Mr. Free Speech must have been terribly disappointed when DNA evidence was presented in the case of Diana's death. It was final proof that Diana was killed not by the hated shutterbugs, but by her alcohol and pill-popping driver, Henri Paul.

Clooney quickly switched his political blathering from photographers to liberal politics. As was evident with his Charlton Heston comments, he simply did not care, or did not recognize, how offensive, or even hurtful, his words can sound.

"What did Bush do on 9/11? He ran away and hid," he told Britain's left-leaning *Guardian* newspaper. "Even Reagan knew more about leadership than that, and he was as bad a symbol of America as I can think of, off-hand. But at least he's been in enough cowboy movies to know he had to come out and stand on top of the rubble and be seen shaking his fist or something."

He went on, "They tell us we're going to war and no one's saying 'Bullsh*t' loud enough. And the language! Listen to the language! 'Evil.' 'Evil'? 'Nexus of evil'? ," Clooney said, mangling the phrase, "axis of evil."

"'Evil-doer'? That's my favorite, 'evil-doer'! What's wrong with their vocabulary: couldn't they come up with 'schmuck'?" railed Clooney.

Clooney told *GQ* magazine that he keeps a photo of his fellow celebutard, ex-President Jimmy Carter, visiting the *ER* set on display in his bathroom. He also thinks Mario Cuomo should be president, and compared Newt Gingrich to a dinosaur. "The man has no arms," he laughed.

> *Clooney told GQ magazine that he keeps a photo of his fellow celebutard, ex-President Jimmy Carter, visiting the ER set on display in his bathroom.*

"The problem is we elected a manager, and we need a leader," Clooney told the magazine. "Let's face it: Bush is just dim."

Pot, kettle? One who demonstrates his own dimness so promiscuously probably should avoid such terms. But I'd never sleep if I allowed myself to take regular offense at the ravings of celebutards. And yet, it's hard to gloss over this classic Clooneyism, which he spilled to German TV: "You can't beat your enemy anymore through wars; instead you create an entire generation of people revenge-seeking. These days, it only matters who's in charge. Right now that's us—for a while at least. Our opponents are going to resort to car bombs and suicide attacks because they have no other way to win."

Did I read that right? Is Clooney suggesting that we and our allies simply stop defending ourselves, so as not to encourage "revenge-seeking"? With these words, Clooney mindlessly excuses the dastardly work of suicide bombers and terrorists, while making us into the bad guys. He grandly espouses what's known as a "rape mentality"—a way of thinking that says, "If you attack me, it's my fault!"

Clooney has brought his lack of intellectual seriousness into such labors of love as *Good Night and Good Luck*, which received generally glowing reviews and bagged six Oscar nominations, including one for best picture and best director, but won nothing on Oscar night. His story that lionizes TV journalist Edward R. Murrow as the guy who took down Commie hunting Senator Joseph McCarthy is historically flawed. In fact, Murrow was decidedly late to the dump-McCarthy party. See how Jack Shafer of *Slate* eviscerated Clooney's movie: "If Jesus Christ no longer satisfies your desire to worship a man as God, I suggest you buy a ticket for *Good Night and Good Luck*, the new movie about legendary CBS News broadcaster Edward R. Murrow. . . . Of course, Murrow was no god. Point of fact, he shouldn't be regarded as the patron saint of broadcast news his fans, among them *Good Night and Good Luck* director George Clooney, make him out to be."

And then there's *Syriana*. That movie takes a book about an attempt by an assassin, played by Clooney, to kill Saddam Hussein—inarguably a very bad man—and changes it into a story about Clooney's attempt to knock off a liberal prince. A good man.

With its confusing plot concentrating on the evil United States government and greedy, amoral oil companies, columnist Charles Krauthammer criticized the movie's distinctly anti-American views. "Osama bin Laden could not have scripted this film with more conviction," he wrote.

Perhaps Clooney should limit his activism to saving Darfur, a movement he brought to prominence on Oprah Winfrey's TV talk show.

But this is not the last we have heard from Clooney, who fully intends to continue making political balderdash—interspersed with money-making movies.

Do I think George Clooney is the sexiest man alive?

As a straight woman with a healthy appetite for handsome men, but an even stronger hunger for thinking for myself, I find the dashing Mr. Clooney highly resistible.

5

They Put the Bull in Durham

SUSAN SARANDON and TIM ROBBINS

You're so lucky in Ireland, England, and Spain. Everyone there already knows what it's like to have inexplicable terrorist violence.

> —Susan Sarandon, on the September 11, 2001, terrorist attacks

When I visit Susan I tread on eggs. . . . I was sitting at the breakfast table with Jack Henry, my then-thirteen-year-old grandson, and he looked over at me with the sweetest little smile on his face and said, 'I hear you voted for Bush.' . . . And I thought, 'I'm not going to discuss my politics with a thirteen-year-old who has been brainwashed!'

> —Susan's mother Lenora Tomalin to the *Washington Post*,
>   March 2003

If you ever write about my family again, I will [bleeping] find you and I will [bleeping] hurt you.

> —Tim Robbins to the *Washington Post*, March 2003

BEWARE THE PACIFISTS.

From the dawn of their unmarried union in 1988, actors Susan Sarandon and Tim Robbins have presented themselves as better informed and made of higher moral fiber than not only the public and, naturally, the government, but blood relatives and friends. As long as leftist causes have existed, the pair has been in the forefront, opposing the death penalty, approving of gay rights, of ending wars, and freeing cop-killer Mumia Abu-Jamal. You might ask how this activity distinguishes them from the countless, mindless celebutards dotting the landscape. It doesn't. But when they speak, the Robbins/Sarandons employ a grating urgency that says, "Shut up! We know better than you." And Susan's mom is a card-carrying Republican.

Something tells me national holidays must be gruesome affairs around the Robbins/ Sarandon dinner table.

Susan Abigail Tomalin was born on October 4, 1946, the eldest of nine children of Lenora and Phillip Tomalin, an advertising executive, television producer and big band-era nightclub singer. The name Sarandon comes from the actress's marriage to actor Chris Sarandon, which lasted from 1967 to 1979.

Timothy Francis Robbins followed Susan into the world twelve years later, on October 16, 1958, in West Covina, California, the son of Mary, an actress, and Gil Robbins, a musician and folk singer. Tim attended the State University of New York at Plattsburgh and finished studies at UCLA's film school, while Sarandon earned a bachelor of arts degree in drama from the Catholic University of America. Though the duo has never wed, their union has produced two sons, born in 1989 and 1992.

Early on, Sarandon was known for playing virginal Janet Weiss, who learns about bisexual lovemaking and naughty lingerie in the 1975 cult film, *The Rocky Horror Picture Show*, and for her groundbreaking onscreen sex scene with French actress Catherine Deneuve in the 1983 vampire flick, *The Hunger*.

But earnest activism would soon overshadow heavy breathing. Robbins' and Sarandon's public and private cause work can be traced at least as far back as the 1995 film *Dead Man Walking*. The anti-death penalty flick was directed by Robbins, and Susan won a best-actress Oscar starring as condemned convict Sean Penn's nun and confessor, Sister Helen Prejean. But it was the terrorist attacks of September 11, 2001, that unleashed the full fury of the Robbins/Sarandons.

In the tense days following, as most of America feared more attacks, President George W. Bush's perhaps inartful declaration, "You're either with us or with the terrorists," was taken personally by the pair, who seemed more concerned with pacifying evil-doers than protecting our soil. They spoke out against the government to anyone who would listen. And then, something strange happened: Nothing.

The couple was geared up for a fight. But they did not find it. No goons came in the night to bop them on the noggin. No one locked them up, shut them up, or kept them under watch. The Hollywood sweethearts continued to find work and to prattle on, unmolested. In truth, they had little to whine about. But that didn't stop them from claiming to be the victims of a vast conspiracy of censorship.

Such was the case in 2003, when Dale Petroskey, president of the Baseball Hall of Fame in Cooperstown, New York, and a former staffer of President Ronald Reagan, canceled an event scheduled to celebrate the fifteenth anniversary of the movie, *Bull Durham*, on which Robbins and Sarandon met. In the film, Sarandon starred as an aging minor-league baseball groupie and Robbins as a player. Petroskey feared the pair's presence at Cooperstown during the difficult dawn of the war in Iraq represented "a danger," and would not gibe with the sensibilities of audience members.

The couple cried "Censorship!"

Wait a minute. Celebutards have this annoying habit: A complete inability to understand basic concepts of law. Or rather, they willfully misrepresent the law, in order to paint themselves as victims. Which is amusing, when you consider how much free publicity the "censored" couple received in the following days.

Robbins held the floor at the National Press Club. "Any instance of intimidation of free speech should be battled against. Any acquiescence to intimidation, at this point, will only lead to more intimidation. Millions are watching and waiting in mute fashion and [are] hoping for someone to defend the spirit and letter of our Constitution and to defy the intimidation that is visited upon us daily in the name of national security and warped notions of patriotism. We must honor and fight vigilantly for the things that unite us. Like freedom, the First Amendment, and, yes, baseball."

For someone complaining about being shut up, Sarandon sure made a lot of noise. She hijacked a CBS *Early Show* interview to talk about the baseball event.

"It's an interesting idea, you know, to say to people, ironic really, since we're supposedly liberating the Iraqis for a democracy and then you're telling people in this country where we have a democracy that you can't have difference of opinion when the very basis for democracy is healthy discourse. I know the American people are not stupid. And I know they believe in democracy in the way I do. And they support their, you know, Bill of Rights."

It was a typical performance. Sarandon and Robbins misrepresented the laws that played into the flap. Let me give a primer on the Constitution 101, since the college-educated couple evidently napped that day in class. The First Amendment prohibits the government from curtailing free speech. There is nothing in the Constitution that guarantees obnoxious celebutards a stage on private property. Nothing.

In a hilarious interview the following June in *Los Angeles Citybeat*, Sarandon gives some clues as to why being prohibited from speaking in

There is nothing in the Constitution that guarantees obnoxious celebutards a stage on private property.

Cooperstown represented no less than a danger to society: She knows more than you do.

"I really see myself as someone who has access to information most people don't get. I am tired of being afraid. I know so many people [at protest rallies] have been talking to me—I was just asking questions other people weren't in the position to ask. I am not leading any movement. I'm just representing voiceless people who, a lot of times, aren't getting the information they need in order to make their own decision."

She never explained from whom she gets the confidential information. Or what it is. Or why it is only available to Susan Sarandon. She did claim to be "right in the middle of it" on 9/11—actually, more than twenty blocks north of the carnage, in Union Square. But she took away from the attacks a message far different than anything gleaned by other witnesses to the atrocities, such as myself.

"I had lost people on that day, and I was hoping that the event would shake us through our complacency and connect us to the world," she told *Citybeat*. "Instead, the president and his honchos missed the opportunity to say, 'We are going to be a stronger country now. We are going to be the best educated. We are going to feed our people. We're going to get real about how we are perceived throughout the rest of the world. There's going to be change in our foreign policy.' [However] the lies, misinformation at best, continued to permeate the news."

Actually, as an American, a New Yorker, and a mom, I was more concerned with stopping the attacks than capitulating to the terrorists, an issue Sarandon did not address. And the attacks did stop. Sorry, Susan.

I suppose no amount of celeb-driven hypocrisy should surprise me. But considering that Susan Sarandon is our nation's self-appointed avatar of free expression, it struck me as bizarre that she summoned the *chutzpah* to urge sponsors to boycott a syndicated television show planned for radio shrink Dr. Laura Schlessinger. Of course, Dr. Laura once called homosexuals a "biological error." That sort of free speech is not allowed.

"I'm totally against wasting the airwaves, giving visibility to a person who is clearly in dire need of compassion, education, and a good shrink herself," Sarandon said in a statement posted on Stop DrLaura.com.

The TV show was canceled in 2001, killed by lack of sponsors, which might be Susan's fault, and plummeting ratings, which was not.

Sometimes, an event so well crystallizes a celebrity's complete inability to see who he is—in this case, a buffoon—that it requires little comment. Such an episode took place in March 2003, after Lloyd Grove, then a gossip columnist for the *Washington Post*, conducted a brief telephone interview with Lenora Tomalin, the then seventy-nine-year-old mother of Susan Sarandon.

"I am a conservative. I voted for George W. Bush and I simply agree with most everything he has said," Mrs. Tomalin told him. "It's not that I'm pro–war. It's just that I think that I trust my government more than I would empathize with the government of Iraq."

She proceeded to talk about Sarandon's views against the president. "That's a given. That's the way she thinks. That's what Hollywood thinks. We don't agree, but I respect her—more than she does me." Pressed on whether her daughter supports Mom's right to an opinion, she replied, "Wanna bet?

"When I visit Susan, I tread on eggs. The most difficult time was during the election of 2000. I live in Florida, and I was a Republican poll-watcher in Polk County. Afterward, I was sitting at the breakfast table with Jack Henry, my then-thirteen-year-old grandson, and he looked over at me, with the sweetest little smile on his face, and said, 'I hear you voted for Bush.' I looked up at Susan, who's standing at the sink, and she says, 'All he wants to know is: How could you have voted for Bush?' And I thought, 'I'm not going to discuss my politics with a thirteen-year-old who has been brainwashed!' But I just let it go—even though I have never been as rabid as I have been during the past few years."

Soon after, the writer showed up at the *Vanity Fair* post–Oscar party, which Robbins also attended. The confrontation between the scribe and the peacenik was as uproarious as it was ugly.

"You're the one who wrote about Susan's mother?" Robbins demanded. "You wanted to be divisive and you caused trouble in my family. If you ever write about my family again, I will f*cking find you and I will f*cking hurt you!"

One wonders if increasing the fiber in Robbins's diet might improve his mood. If Tim Robbins does not want Grandma, an adult, blabbing to the press, particularly about his young son, it seems a subject best taken up with the woman, and not dealt with by threatening violence against a reporter who was, after all, just doing his job. Such valiant protection of those nearest and dearest did not prevent Robbins from soon exploiting another young family member.

Less than three weeks after the Lenora flap, Robbins told the National Press Club, "A relative tells me that a history teacher tells his eleven-year-old son, my nephew, that Susan Sarandon is endangering the troops by her opposition to the war." But the alarming tale ended on a note of Robbins-style triumph.

He said his nephew, normally a quiet lad, stood up in class and declared, "That's my aunt you're talking about. Stop it."

For the Robbins/Sarandons, all stories end peacefully. If not, they'll hurt you.

6

Chumps Like Us

BRUCE SPRINGSTEEN

Tramps like us, baby we were born to run.
—Bruce Springsteen's "Born to Run," 1975

Over the past six years we've had to add to the American picture: rendition, illegal wiretapping, voter suppression, no habeas corpus, the neglect of our great city New Orleans and its people, an attack on the Constitution. And the loss of our young best men and women in a tragic war. This is a song about things that shouldn't happen here—happening here.
—Springsteen on the *Today* show, September 2007

I USED TO BELIEVE IN Bruce Springsteen. I also used to believe in the Tooth Fairy, the Easter Bunny, and Hanukkah Harry. But growing into adulthood I learned, to my great dismay, that each is as illusory as Barry Bonds' home run record.

To legions of fans in his native New Jersey and around the world, Springsteen evoked a kind of stoic wisdom as a latter-day Joe Lunch Bucket, singing about the sounds, the sweat and the teen

43

age angst above and below the boardwalk at Asbury Park on the New Jersey shore. What a surprise to learn that it's all an act, and Springsteen is just another big-mouth celebrity twit eager to share whatever fashionable leftist political nonsense enters his none-too-swift brain.

I grew up a Springsteen fan in simpler days, when the man known as The Boss sang directly to the disaffected youth of America, which was just about all of us, about getting high, getting laid and getting a job. That is, he directed his energies and considerable talents toward meditations on subjects about which he knew something.

WHO CAN RESIST "Rosalita (Come Out Tonight)," recorded in 1973, an ode to raw sex and skipping school, featuring characters known as Sloppy Sue and Big Bones Billy.

But twenty-seven years later, every police officer in the city of New York, Springsteen's natural constituency, would feel as if they were stabbed in the back with the release of Springsteen's angry song about the tragic, but completely unintentional, shooting of African immigrant Amadou Diallo, "American Skin (41 Shots)": The song features a mother with a decidedly Hispanic name, who advises her son to obey police officers, always keeping his hands in sight. It was not meant as sound advice from one law-abiding citizen to another, but rather the song was a deep dig at cops. Springsteen, by now ensconced in a mansion, imagined that the police were bent on shooting innocent youth. He issued no similar song on behalf of police.

THE SPRINGSTEEN I thought I knew would have identified with the police, understood they put their lives on the line, every day, to save his hide. But those days were over. With this song, in my opinion, and others to follow, he proved that his image of a struggling, all-American working guy—a pose that made him rich—was carefully honed in a publicist's office, not a factory. The only sweat

Springsteen ever expended was over the size of his royalties. He should have quit with *Born in the USA.*

Bruce Frederick Joseph Springsteen was born September 23, 1949, in Long Branch, New Jersey. The name Springsteen is Dutch, his background Roman Catholic, though Adam Sandler (so far not a celebutard) poked fun at him in his second "Hanukkah Song" with the line, "Bruce Springsteen isn't Jewish, but my mother thinks he is."

Like many creative types, Springsteen did not fit into school as a child, despising the cruelty he encountered in Catholic education, where he said a nun once stuffed him into a garbage can under the desk. Transferring to public school, he also failed to fit in, skipping his high school graduation ceremony. He attended Ocean County College briefly, before dropping out. So much for formal education.

Legend has it that he bought his first guitar for $18.00 at age thirteen. In 1965, he started singing with a band called The Castiles, then in the early '70s with a group that would later be called The E Street Band. He signed his first record contract in 1972, putting out the critically acclaimed, but initially not very well noticed, *Greetings From Asbury Park, N.J.* and *The Wild, the Innocent and the E Street Shuffle.* He would not struggle long. It was clear his career was to take off like a bullet when this famous rave review by Jon Landau appeared in Boston's *The Real Paper* in 1974: "I saw rock and roll future and its name is Bruce Springsteen. On a night when I needed to feel young, he made me feel like I was hearing music for the very first time."

In 1975, Springsteen had his first commercial success with *Born to Run.* The week it was released, he appeared on the covers of both *Time* and *Newsweek.* A career was launched.

Springsteen recorded perhaps his most famous album, *Born in the U.S.A.*, in 1984, appearing on the record jacket in blue jeans with an American flag. The album railed against the ill treatment by some segments of society against Vietnam War veterans, Springsteen's friends and band mates, but did not explicitly make a political statement on the war itself. During his *Born in the U.S.A.* tour he met Julianne Phillips, an actress and model, whom he wed in 1985. New Jersey went into shock.

A virtual state of emergency was declared, so appalled were Springsteen's ardent fans that Bruce had "gone Hollywood." Why, his wife wasn't even from the Garden State! She looked more comfortable tooling around in limousines than on the back of a motorcycle. Fans feared that Mrs. Springsteen might break a nail if she attempted to change a tire.

But Springsteen filed for divorce from Phillips in 1988, and moved into a relationship with Patti Scialfa, a Jersey girl and back up singer with Springsteen's E Street Band (Phillips was said to learn about the relationship by reading the tabloids.) Scialfa gave birth to the first of Springsteen's three children in 1990, and married him the next year. New Jersey heaved a heavy sigh of relief. *Time* magazine encapsulated The Boss's betrayal to his home state, and seeming return to the fold, thusly: "So after a failed marriage to model-actress Julianne Phillips, Springsteen moved into a $14 million mansion in Beverly Hills (the faithful jeered), wed Scialfa in 1991 (the faithful cheered) and sang about relationships, kids and his ennui (the faithful shrugged)."

In hindsight, the criticism lavished on Phillips wasn't fair. Bruce Springsteen was more than capable of going Hollywood with a Jersey girl at his side.

Springsteen moved back to New Jersey with his family in the mid-1990s, taking up principal residence in an estate in Rumson, one of the poshest towns in the state. If his music at times had grown moody and introverted, it was about to become politically extroverted. This was not the Bruce we knew.

In 1999 Amadou Diallo, a 23-year-old West African immigrant, was shot to death in the Bronx by four white police officers, all terrified for their lives. The police, who encountered Diallo in a dark doorway, thought he was pulling out a gun when, in reality, he pulled out a wallet. It turned out Diallo was unarmed.

The officers fired at Diallo forty-one times, striking him with nineteen bullets. It was a tragedy. But it was a mistake. The officers were indicted on charges of second-degree murder and a trial was held upstate, in Albany, New York. I have long remembered this column written by *New York Times* op-ed columnist Bob Herbert, an African-American liberal firebrand, because it reeks of common sense: "The killing of Amadou Diallo was cold-blooded, but it probably wasn't murder. It appears that one or more of the officers genuinely believed Mr. Diallo had a gun and that all four officers, imagining danger when in fact there was none, panicked and began firing.

"There is no doubt that the shooting was reckless and wrong. The forty-one shots from the frightened cops turned a terrible mistake into a hideous one. But even a hideous mistake by police officers who think their lives are in danger falls short of the threshold for second-degree murder."

Albany jurors agreed with Bob Herbert, and in 2000 found the four police officers not guilty of all charges. But noted police scholar Bruce Springsteen held a different view. He performed "American Skin (41 Shots)," a song with upsetting, hypnotic lyrics that build in intensity, and reach a climax with the assurance that a person can get slaughtered by police. Just for "living in your American skin."

The song brought heavy condemnation from New York City Mayor Rudolph Giuliani and Police Commissioner Howard Safir. Hundreds of police held anti-Springsteen protests, and Patrolmen's Benevolent Association President Patrick Lynch wrote to his membership: "I consider it an outrage that he would be trying to fatten his wallet by reopening the wounds of this tragic case at a time when police officers and community members are in a healing period." He urged city cops to boycott Springsteen's shows.

The New York Times' token conservative columnist at the time, John Tierney, wrote: "Mr. Springsteen is no longer the poor

Jersey kid singing about his blue-collar neighbors. He is a million-aire who doesn't have to hitchhike on Route 9 anymore. The singer who once defended Vietnam veterans and Middle American values has lately been focused on conventional liberal causes, like home-lessness and AIDS."

In the wake of the terrorist attacks of September 11, 2001, Bruce found good use for his international platform. Initially, he hit the "pause" button on his political speeches, but only briefly. This gave him time to cash in on the worst attack in United States his-tory. Yes, September 11 was good to Bruce.

The Rising was released in 2002, a sad, moody album, not acutely political. It is true that no one owns 9/11, and many artists have profited from the carnage. But for Springsteen, who'd decided that police were killers and the war against terror was bloodthirsty and unjust, it angered me no end that he felt he had the right to ex-ploit the attacks for personal and professional gain.

In a TV interview promoting the album, I watched Springsteen field a seemingly innocuous question: Where did you spend that dreadful day? Springsteen paused for a split second, before replying that he hunkered down in his fancy mansion, and watched the at-tacks on TV.

I spent the days after September 11 around the smoldering pile in lower Manhattan, trying to help a family search for their loved one, a young husband and father named Paul Ortiz. For days, his beautiful family prayed that somehow he survived. After days of searching, it was clear he had not. His young wife thanked me for my devotion. Such kindness was humbling. I had done nothing.

I was far from alone. Thousands of men and women volunteered to dig through the rubble, to help in any way they could. Spring-steen must have felt he was helping someone. But bashing the gov-ernment for starting a war that, the administration hoped, would prevent future terrorist attacks helped no one. Except maybe Bruce Springsteen.

In October 2003, Bruce Springsteen took the stage at Shea Stadium for *The Rising* tour. Just before launching into "Souls of the Departed," a song about U.S. soldiers in Iraq, he urged the crowd to shout "a little louder if you want to impeach the president."

A letter-writer to the *New York Post* who attended the concert informed readers that "droves of people" ripped up their tickets, booed and shouted obscenities at Springsteen, then walked out of the show.

It was reported in 2006 that Springsteen's life was affected by 9/11 in another way: the star was said to have grown close to a redhead, not his wife. She was a widow Springsteen met while organizing a charity event for survivors of the terrorist attacks. But Springsteen responded to the rumors of marital discord, posting this on his personal Web site: "Due to the unfounded and ugly rumors that have appeared in the papers of the last few days, I felt they shouldn't pass without comment. Patti and I have been together for eighteen years—the best eighteen years of my life. We have built a beautiful family we love and want to protect and our commitment to one another remains as strong as the day we were married."

If there remained any question what side Springsteen was on, he put it to rest with the release of *Magic* the next year.

"This is a song called 'Livin' in the Future.' But it's really about what's happening now. Right now. It's kind of about how the things we love about America, cheeseburgers, French fries, the Yankees battlin' Boston, the Bill of Rights, V-twin motorcycles, Tim Russert's

> *A letter-writer to the New York Post who attended the concert informed readers that "droves of people" ripped up their tickets, booed and shouted obscenities at Springsteen, then walked out of the show.*

haircut, trans-fats and the Jersey Shore. . . . We love those things the way womenfolk love on Matt Lauer.

"But over the past six years we've had to add to the American picture: rendition, illegal wiretapping, voter suppression, no habeas corpus, the neglect of that great city New Orleans and its people, an attack on the Constitution. And the loss of our best men and women in a tragic war.

"This is a song about things that shouldn't happen here happening here."

From trans-fats, of which he evidently approves, to rendition, illegal wiretapping, etc., all of which he apparently does not.

And then, he sang.

I'd already changed the channel.

7

The Bimbo Summit

PARIS, BRITNEY, and LINDSAY

What is Wal-Mart? Is it, like, they sell walls?
—Paris Hilton on *The Simple Life*

The cool thing about being famous is traveling. I have always wanted to travel across seas, like to Canada and stuff.
—Britney Spears on the road

I am lucky enough to of been able to work with Robert Altman amongst the other greats on a film I can genuinely say created a turning point in my career. He was the closest thing to my father and grandfather that I really do believe I've had in several years. . . .
—Lindsay Lohan on the director's death

BEAT POET ALLEN GINSBERG wrote in *Howl*—"I saw the best minds of my generation destroyed by madness, starving hysterical naked . . ."
With apologies to Mr. Ginsberg, I amend that sentiment:

"I saw the feeblest minds of my generation destroyed by drugs, anonymous sex, illiteracy. Bingeing, puking hysterical dead."

It's been said that a nation gets the government it deserves. The same can be said about celebutards. Still, a mystery that sometimes keeps me awake at night, at least until the Ambien kicks in, is this: What awful crime must the people of the United States have committed to ensure that, several years into the millennium, the three most famous people in this country, if not on the entire planet, are named Britney, Lindsay, and Paris?

We may never know what we did to deserve them, but stuck with them we are. As long as a girl child bares her navel or bears neglected children to emulate Britney Spears, we must pay attention. As long as a youngster enters rehab before reaching the age of twenty-one, à la Lindsay Lohan, we can't forget. And so long as a child exhibits no ambition other than to be ushered in to the VIP section of the hottest nightclub, or perhaps receive infection from genital herpes, as Paris Hilton, we don't dare look away.

In November 2006, the world as we know it ended. That was the night the three bimbos of the apocalypse joined forces. Paris, Britney, and Lindsay hit the scene in Los Angeles, clubbing all night in a fury of estrogen and anti-inflammatory drugs, a scene summed up by a memorable *New York Post* headline, "Bimbo Summit."

Britney, sans underwear, was photographed, repeatedly, in all her post-partum delicacy, her inflamed C-section scar clearly visible under a skirt so short, she shouldn't have bothered. Soon, her antics would rival her more experienced rivals' for sheer insanity.

In the coming months, these women, in turn, would get their mug shots taken (Paris, Lindsay), two would flirt with rehab (Britney, Lindsay), and one would see her children taken from her incompetent clutches (Britney).

All three would claim, at one time or another, to have gone straight. They would be less than convincing.

PARIS

Paris Whitney Hilton was born in New York City on February 17, 1981, an heiress to the Hilton hotel fortune. Her acting credits include co-starring with fellow celebrity slug Nicole Richie on a reality show, *The Simple Life*, depicting a spoiled, skinny starlet who wreaks havoc across America, as she talks sexually to impressionable children, and screws up every job she tries. That is, she was typecast as herself.

She told Britain's *Sunday Times* in 2006, "I think every decade has an iconic blonde—like Marilyn Monroe or Princess Diana—and right now, I'm that icon."

The idea of holding up a single female to represent a generation is as old as celebrity itself. Each age honors women who were usually blond and more than likely dumb. In the '50s and '60s it was Paris's idol, Marilyn Monroe. In the '90s, it was Princess Diana. But Paris is no Marilyn or Diana. She's not even a convincing impersonator.

While Monroe demonstrated genuine acting talent, Paris has displayed ability only for being pampered, petulant, and engaging in strenuous sexual intercourse on a much-downloaded video that shows Paris performing the nasty with a fellow named Rick Salomon. And while Diana expertly manipulated the media—no mean feat when you're locked up, miserable, in a dank palace—the only shackles Paris ever wore were those she slipped into on her own, kinky accord.

Of course, the irony is that in the fearful downgrading of celebrity that is honored today, the Paris Hilton sex tape was enough. It turned our useless heiress into an international sensation.

Paris has never earned a seat at the banquet table occupied by the late, great blondes, Marilyn and Diana. It is testament to her idiocy that she doesn't know the difference. It is testament to society's collective lunacy that Paris is so famous.

I have proof. One day in early 2007, I decided to make a terribly unscientific survey of the relative fame of Paris Hilton. To do this, I took full-color photographs of two celebrated women—Paris Hilton and Associate Supreme Court Justice Ruth Bader Ginsburg—into the Bed, Bath & Beyond store on Sixth Avenue in Manhattan. Full disclosure: I needed to buy towels.

It came with great disappointment, and virtually no surprise, that almost everyone recognized Paris—with the exception of two Hasidic women, who looked scared when I approached with my pictures in hand. Practically every New Yorker in my random survey came up not only with Paris Hilton's first and last names, but they knew that she lived in California, and that she was known mainly for going to parties, and lived on Mommy and Daddy's money, a factoid Paris vehemently denies.

"She doesn't do anything except go to clubs and hang out," said Tara Serrano, age seventeen.

"She seems like she had too much given to her in life," said Regina Pegg, age thirty-four.

But only one man in all of Manhattan, store manager Keith Goldberg, was able to pick Ruth out of a lineup.

In coming months, Paris would get even more famous, although it probably was not what she had in mind.

In January 2007, Paris's personal stuff—diaries and notes, naked photos, even a prescription for the herpes medication, Valtrex—was purchased at auction for a measly $2,775, after Paris failed to pay a $208 storage bill. "I love shoes," read one vapid note in the heiress's hand. Another talked of performing oral sex with her former fiance, Jason Shaw. She is heard wielding ethnic slurs, including the so-called "N" word, in footage included among the collection, whose contents were viewed, like an electronic peep show, on the Internet.

But even that seeming lapse in dignity would be eclipsed in May 2007. That day, a Los Angeles judge made history. He sentenced Paris to forty-five days in jail.

The sentence was for a traffic stop the previous September, in which she'd failed a sobriety test. The next January, she pleaded no contest to a charge of reckless driving. Displaying either a complete lack of regard to the rule of law, or proof that she did not possess two brain cells to rub together, she was subsequently stopped behind the wheel—twice—while her license was suspended. The first time, cops had Paris sign a document acknowledging she was prohibited from operating a motor car. The second time she was picked up, she had her lights off. The smoking document was in her glove compartment.

Her excuse? She said she never read it. She hired people to read for her. She blamed her publicist, Elliot Mintz, for telling her it was okay to drive. She blamed her pathetic excuse for a dog, nitwit Chihuahua Tinkerbell. Everyone was to blame, except herself.

To the thrill of much of America, and certainly its motorists and vulnerable pedestrians, Judge Michael T. Sauer was to make an example, and prove that, in his court, even in the notoriously fame-friendly state of California, a celebrity might be treated like anyone else. Paris's sentence was already reduced on Day One to twenty-three days. This was still too harsh for Paris's well-heeled parents, Kathy and Rick Hilton.

Paris's mom taunted the judge on sentencing day, "May I have your autograph?" And when she approached

There were conflicting reports as to whether she was able to skip the standard body-cavity search, though it was unclear whether this was due to her fame, or to the difficulty of finding someone willing to perform the deed.

the bench, Kathy was blocked by a court officer. "You touched my breast!" she squealed like a banshee. As if.

In June, Paris was booked into the Century Regional Detention Center with extreme swiftness, as Paris does not wish to wait in line. There were conflicting reports as to whether she was able to skip the standard body-cavity search, though it was unclear whether this was due to her fame, or to the difficulty of finding someone willing to perform the deed.

But just three days later, Paris was back on the streets. She was freed by Los Angeles County Sheriff Lee Baca, a buddy of celebs such as Mel Gibson, who claimed Paris had to be switched to house arrest because she was suffering an "imminent breakdown." So much for the rule of law.

Judge Sauer hit the roof.

The judge ordered Paris back into his courtroom immediately. There, he told her she would serve the rest of her sentence, behind bars. No mansion. No parties. No whining. As he did so, Paris wailed, "Mommmmm! It's not fair!" And back to jail Paris went.

She was released, finally, on June 26, 2007, after serving twenty-two days, including her single day at home. So tell me, Paris, what have you learned?

Paris wore a matronly, lacy top for her coming-out interview with Larry King, where she presented herself as reformed—and a victim. In one breath, she mumbled that her sentence was unfair. In another, she said it was the best thing to ever happen to her. She denied she was an alcoholic. She said she never did drugs. And she vowed to help women in prison in some vague way.

But then Larry King, who seemed to have lost interest in his subject along the way, inadvertently tripped her up. Paris told him she read the Bible non-stop behind bars. So he asked, "What's your favorite Bible passage?"

Paris looked frightened. She stalled. Then she said, "I don't have a favorite, but . . ."

"You read it every day?" Larry asked, incredulously. Paris answered, weakly, "In jail, I read a lot."

Within a few days she was back on the party circuit.

Maybe she'll use a driver from now on.

LINDSAY

Born on July 2, 1986, Lindsay Dee Lohan is the baby of this unholy association, though she runs a good race for the title of World's Most Troubled Starlet.

She was born in the Bronx and raised on Long Island, New York, to mother Dina, who has long claimed to be a former Rockette. But the Rockettes have no record of Dina ever dancing for them, nor do they know a Donata Sullivan, as she was once known. One thing is certain, mom Dina has long competed for her actress daughter's fame, as was evident in the April 2007 issue of *Harper's Bazaar*, in which she revealed she sometimes introduces herself as her daughter's personal assistant. She even lied about her identity to actor George Clooney.

"I don't want them to know I'm her mom," she said. "It's a whole 'nother demographic. People just go dark."

Her father, Michael, was sentenced to four years in prison for securities fraud in the late 1980s, and spent much of his daughter's teen years behind bars. He was sent back to prison for nearly two years in 2005 for aggravated unlicensed driving and attempted assault. Given a choice, I guess Michael wins the title of worst role model. Lindsay's parents are divorced.

Lindsay started acting as a child, and quickly developed into a freckle-faced breath of fresh air, playing wholesome girls with good heads on their shoulders in such films as *Freaky Friday* and *Herbie: Fully Loaded*. The camera did not divulge what lay beneath.

Billionaire and professional celeb pal Brandon Davis gave Lindsay a name that has stuck to her, like a worm to a bottle of tequila. He called her "Firecrotch."

Long before she hit the legal drinking age of twenty-one, Lilo, as I think of her, was on the booze. In July 2006, the head of the company producing Lindsay's flick, *Georgia Rule*, wrote her a blistering letter complaining about her all-night partying and frequent sick calls.

"To date, your actions on *Georgia Rule* have been discourteous, irresponsible and unprofessional," wrote Morgan Creek's chief executive officer, James G. Robinson. "You have acted like a spoiled child and in doing so have alienated many of your co-workers and endangered the quality of *Georgia Rule*." He advised her to take heed. She should have listened.

Her words can be hard to take, painful even, but march through them we must—if only to demonstrate that proper education, good nutrition, and sufficient sleep are paramount to the healthy growth of young women.

I think the best way to know Lilo is through her own, incoherent, written ramblings. Her words can be hard to take, painful even, but march through them we must—if only to demonstrate that proper education, good nutrition, and sufficient sleep are paramount to the healthy growth of young women.

Here, then, is the letter Lindsay released to the family of director Robert Altman upon his death in November 2006. Punctuation, spelling and grammar are Lindsay's:

"I would like to send my condolences out to Catherine Altman, Robert Altmans wife, as well as all of his immediate family, close friends, co-workers, and all of his inner circle.

"I feel as if I've just had the wind knocked out of me and my heart aches . . .

"I learned so much from Altman and he was the closest thing

to my father and grandfather that I really do believe I've had in several years.

"Look in the mirror and thank god for every second you have and cherish all moments.

"The fighting, the anger, the drama is tedious.

"Please just take each moment day by day and consider yourself lucky to breathe and feel at all and smile. Be thankful.

"Make a searching and fearless moral inventory of yourselves' (12st book)—everytime there's a triumph in the world a million souls hafta be trampled on.-altman Its true. But treasure each triumph as they come.

"God Bless, peace and love always.

"Thank You,

" 'BE ADEQUITE'

"Lindsay Lohan"

Good gracious—there is more.

Even as Hollywood collectively reeled from this letter, Lindsay did it again—sending this e-mail to pals and associates barely a month later. You'd believe Lindsay would have learned to think before she hit "send." At the very least, she might look up the spelling of "adequate." Here it is:

"Subject: The way of the future-Howard Hughes once said. I am willing to release a politically/morally correct, fully adequite letter to the press if any of you are willing to help. Simply to state my oppinions on how our society should be educated on for the better of our country. Our people. Also because I have such an impact on our younger generations, as well as generations older than me. Which we all know and can obviously see. People are just mean . . . People cannot lie and think that it is okay to continue on having done so. Simply because they will do it again to someone else, and that is not alright with me. Al Gore will help me. . . .

(Asked if he had promised to help little Lindsay, the former Veep had no clue what she was talking about.) "If he is willing to help me, let's find out. Hilary Clinton, Bill Clinton, and Evan metroplis, and John Daur who works with them would be willing, if we just ask. If we just ASK. I'd really like to fix things and refuse to stop on any account for these unintelligent, vulgar people who like to hurt other people. Not just me, but everyone. I'm willing to hold a press conference and I will do anything necessary to do so. In putting an end to 'these people' trying to put an end to me and belittle me as well as try to be the demise of me after all I've gone through and done at such a young and tender age in a womans life . . . So let's start now, rather than waste time. Do you agree? Because I'm doing it either way. The way of the future. Thank you for your time. Your Entertainer, Lindsay Lohan Sent wirelessly via BlackBerry from T-Mobile."

In the annals of celebutardom, Memorial Day weekend, 2007 stands out as most memorable. That is, if Lindsay can remember it at all.

Still the tender age of twenty, she was popped for drunken driving after crashing her Mercedes against a curb in Los Angeles, where cops recovered what they termed a "usable amount" of cocaine in her jeans. She would later say she did not know whose jeans she was wearing. Later that weekend, in a photograph beamed to newspapers throughout the globe, Lindsay was seen in her SUV outside a Hollywood nightclub at 3 A.M., wearing a gray sweatshirt, fast asleep, with her mouth agape.

She checked into Promises, a spa-like, celebrity-friendly drug and alcohol rehabilitation establishment in Malibu, California, where she quietly spent her twenty-first birthday. But fresh out of rehab, her assistant quit, and Lindsay grew enraged. She proceeded to commandeer an SUV in which three men were sitting, and allegedly took off, speeding, through Los Angeles. When she was stopped by cops, the men claimed she shouted, "I wasn't driving. The black kid was driving."

Like Paris before her, Lindsay was shipped to the Century Regional Detention Center—for eighty-four minutes, not even long enough to drive there on the freeway. At least she beat Nicole Richie, who was shipped to jail for driving under the influence, and spent eighty-two minutes behind bars.

Lindsay followed this act by posing naked for a 2008 *New York* magazine spread, in which she was done up to look like poor-man's Marilyn Monroe. At age twenty-one, she looked strangely worn. And far older than her years.

In the spring of 2008, Lindsay was spotted canoodling with celeb D.J. Samantha Ronson, fueling rumors that she had crossed over to the other side. Mom Dina was fine with it, calling Ronson "a sweetheart."

BRITNEY

How could a girl go so wrong?

Britney Jean Spears was born December 2, 1981, in Mississippi and raised in Kentwood, Louisiana. From a young age, her talent was evident. She was cast as a Mouseketeer on Disney TV's *The Mickey Mouse Club* before the age of thirteen. She then embarked on a successful career as a pop singer, recording such hits as "Oops, I Did It Again."

Oops. She sure did it again. And again. And again.

Britney told anyone who asked, or didn't, that she intended to remain a virgin until marriage, a vow she apparently broke with fellow Mouseketeer Justin Timberlake. Or perhaps it was the night she and Madonna engaged in an open-mouth kiss onstage at the *MTV Video Music Awards* in 2003, in full view of Madge's husband and daughter.

But the first sign of true trouble arrived in January 2004, when an unhinged Britney ran off to Vegas with her high school beau, Jason Alexander, and married him. That union lasted all of fifty-five hours before it was annulled.

Later that year, she announced her pending engagement to

Kevin Federline, an aspiring rapper with no visible means of support. Trouble was, he was in a relationship with Shar Jackson, who at that moment was eight months pregnant with his second child. But love, or more likely, money, trumped all, and the pair were wed in September 2004. A year later, their son, Sean Preston, was born. That was followed the next year with the birth of son Jayden James.

Oh, Britney.

Her skills as a mother, or lack thereof, would soon overshadow everything she had accomplished. Her poor choices in men, in wardrobe, in hair extensions, coupled by her seeming inability to engage a competent publicist, would soon become the stuff of late-night guffaws.

In February 2006, Britney was photographed cruising on the Pacific Coast Highway with baby Sean Preston sitting on her lap, rather than the car seat that any brood mare knows is required by law. This was followed by Sean's April fall from a high chair, in which he banged his head, and earned Britney a visit from child-welfare officials and a sheriff's deputy. In New York, with Sean in one arm, she snapped the kid's neck back and nearly dropped him while successfully preventing a drink from spilling out of the other hand. Priorities.

Still, a defiant Britney—pregnant, snapping gum and wearing ratty hair extensions—appeared on *Dateline: NBC* in June, where she explained her driving lapse to Matt Lauer like this:

"We're country!"

K-Fed was nowhere to be seen.

Nothing was ever the same for Britney after Jayden's birth. Doubtless, for anyone else in the clan. Because immediately upon giving birth, Britney dropped her drawers. She was seen all over Los Angeles in the company of her apocalyptic mates, Paris and Lindsay.

In November 2006, Britney filed for divorce from her "country" hubby. Federline expected alimony from Britney. Within a few months, he'd be entitled to child support as well.

At this point, Britney-watching turned from harmless fun into something like watching open-heart surgery. Without anesthesia. Where in the world were this sick girl's parents?

At this point, Britney-watching turned from harmless fun into something like watching open-heart surgery. Without anesthesia.

Where was any adult?

In February 2007, after skipping out of a drive-by rehab center, Britney staged a public meltdown. Actually, meltdown is too gentle a word. She became horrifically, cataclysmically unglued.

First, she entered a Los Angeles hair salon, where she asked the attendant to shave her head. When the stylist balked, Britney grabbed the shears and did it herself. Next, she visited a tattoo parlor and got herself inked as the cameras rolled. She was staging a planetary cry for help, but there was no one to hear.

Britney, bald and visibly nuts, next was photographed attacking the paparazzi with an umbrella she wielded like a javelin. In July 2007, *OK!* magazine took the unprecedented step of printing an article detailing a disastrous photo shoot, in which Britney wiped her fried chicken-grease covered hands on a $274 dress and picked up her puppy's poop with a $6,700 Zac Posen gown. Britney then was said to flee the shoot wearing $12,861 worth of jewelry, a $974 Vera Wang dress, $380 Lanvin heels and a $281 Pucci scarf. Rock bottom was rushing up to greet her.

Los Angeles Superior Court Commissioner Scott Gordon is a patient man. He gave Britney umpteen chances to undergo random drug testing and to see a parenting coach. But despite all her chances, she failed to comply. She wouldn't even take his calls.

In September 2007, Gordon labeled Britney a "habitual, frequent and continuous" user of alcohol and drugs. Ouch. Early the next month, the kids were taken from her, and handed to her ex, Federline. Her last moments with the kids were spent in typical fashion—Britney took them to a fast-food drive-through window. In the irony that often goes hand-in-hand with celebrity, in this company, the sponge-like K-Fed looked like Father of the Year.

Britney seemed determined to blow her shot at a comeback. Sleep-walking, unrehearsed, through the MTV Video Music Awards in Vegas, the formerly fresh-faced starlet looked bloated in a black, sequined bikini. It was painful to watch.

In January 2008, Britney lost it completely. This time, she threatened to take others with her.

After a visit with her sons, she was to return the boys to their dad. Instead she grabbed hysterical Jayden James, pulled him into a bathroom, and locked the door, keeping him inside the room for three hours as powerless authorities tried to coax her out. Federline said he was scared; he'd given Britney a gun for her birthday. The judge forbade Britney from seeing her children.

Proving that her parents are the dumbest Hillbillies in creation, they initially called not Britney, but Dr. Phil McGraw. Dr. Phil held a press conference to say that Britney was in trouble. Ya think?

Finally, her dad took over legal conservatorship—finally!—distanced Britney from her friends, enablers and lovers, and got her locked in UCLA Medical Center's psychiatric ward.

She was released after six days.

One last note, if you can stand it. Just before Christmas 2007 Britney's little sister, Jamie Lynn, found an odd way to upstage her more famous sister. She announced she was pregnant by her boyfriend at the age of sixteen—too young to legally drink alcohol or drive her kid home from the hospital in some states. And too young to legally have sex with her man, Casey Aldridge, eighteen, who risked statutory rape charges.

The revelation sent shock waves through publishing circles. Mom Lynne Spears' book on, of all things, how to be a celebrity parent, was abruptly canceled, and she said she'd raise her daughter's baby. Scary, when you consider what a fine job Lynne did for her own two girls. Meanwhile, the cable TV channel Nickelodeon struggled over how to handle the baby's baby bump on Jamie Lynn's kiddie show, *Zoey 101*. And moms like me worried about how to explain to our daughters why they should read books rather than take life lessons from the likes of Lindsay, Paris, Britney and Jamie Lynn Spears.

Parents, I beg you. Don't let your babies grow up to be celebutards.

8

All I Wanna Do Is Have Some Dumb
SHERYL CROW

I propose a limitation be put on how many squares of
toilet paper can be used in any one sitting . . . I think we
are an industrious enough people that we can make it
work with only one square per restroom visit, except, of
course, on those pesky occasions where two to three
could be required.
　　—Sheryl Crow's Weblog, April 20, 2007

IT SURE DIDN'T SOUND like a joke. A joke would require a sense of humor.

One day in April 2007, the very earnest, serious, and deeply annoying singer Sheryl Crow made a point on the Web about waste, global warming and all manner of business near and dear to her celebutard heart. But rather than being taken seriously, her illiterate ramblings on combating pollution caused her to become the butt of ridicule and late-night TV jokes.

In a posting entitled, "Apr 19th Stop Global Warming College Tour: Sheryl and Laurie" (that would be Laurie David, environmentalist ex-wife of *Seinfeld* creator Larry David) "Go to School," Sheryl crowed to fans of her elevator-style music: "I have spent the better part of this tour trying to come up with easy ways for us all to become a part of the solution to global warming. Although my ideas are in the earliest stages of development, they are, in my mind, worth investigation. One of my favorites is the idea of conserving trees which we heavily rely on for oxygen. I propose a limitation be put on how many sqares [sic] of toilet paper can be used at any one sitting. Now, I don't want to rob any law-abiding American of his or her God-given rights, but I think we are an industrious enough people that we can make it work with only one square per restroom visit, except, of course, on those pesky occasions where two to three could be required. When presenting this idea to my younger brother, who's [sic] judgement [sic] I trust implicitly, he proposed taking it one step further. I believe his quote was, 'how bout just washing the one square out.'"

Sheryl also liked the idea of not using paper napkins, which, she claimed, were made from virgin wood and represented the "heighth [sic] of wastefullness [sic]." She designed a clothing line called a "dining sleeve." The design offered "the diner the convenience of wiping his mouth on his sleeve rather than throwing out yet another barely used paper product." Always on the ball, Crow also added, "I think this idea could also translate quite well to those suffering with an annoying head cold."

She later said it was a joke designed to get attention. It did. One thing is true: Sheryl Crow is designing a clothing line. So far, there's been no word from the singer about the wasteful duplication of human resources which results when recording artists double up as fashion designers.

Sheryl Suzanne Crow was born February 11, 1962, in Kennett, Missouri, the third of four children born to Wendell Crow, a trumpet player and lawyer, and Bernice, a piano teacher. Sheryl was a cheerleader and athlete in high school and received a bachelor's degree at the University of Missouri, before becoming an elementary school teacher by day who worked on her music career at night. Crow's first major break came when she toured with Michael Jackson during his *BAD* world tour in the late 1980s. She finally hit it huge on her own with her 1993 album *Tuesday Night Music Club*, containing some of her biggest hits. She followed it with a self-titled album that delved into standard political ditties, about homelessness, abortion and nuclear war.

The public first learned the extent of Crow's severe case of celebutardisty when, during the televised 2003 American Music Awards, she came onstage twice wearing a T-shirt bearing the message, "War is not the answer." Crow explained her political statement this way to reporters: "I think war is never the answer to solving any problems. The best way to solve problems is to not have enemies."

> *"I think war is never the answer to solving any problems. The best way to solve problems is to not have enemies."*

Sheryl, think it through! Are you trying to say that all "problems"—including terror attacks against American citizens—were brought on by ourselves because we provoked our enemies? I'm always astonished by the mindless sloganeering of famous folks. I guess if we just capitulate to enemies, disregard our freedoms, turn our back on our friends around the world, maybe slap on burqas for good measure, the bad guys will simply leave us alone to a world filled with Sheryl Crow Muzak.

In addition to Crow's usually innocuous, occasionally pleasant, and always unchallenging music, she is best known for her romance with and engagement to Tour de France-winning cyclist Lance Armstrong, which started in 2003. It didn't seem to calm her down, however. Crow was singing at a corporate event at Cipriani's in New York when a witness heard her loudly going on about Lance. "Lance and I this, Lance and I that," the witness said. Then, she cruelly threw out of the building the dish washers, servers and their children, who'd gathered since early morning for a peek at their idol.

But Armstrong broke off his engagement with Crow after she was diagnosed with early-stage breast cancer in February 2006.

Armstrong, himself a survivor of testicular cancer, confessed to *Men's Journal* about his difficulty handling her disease. (He is also rumored to be a supporter of President Bush.) The twin crises—diagnosis of a serious disease and the end of what was supposed to be a permanent relationship—did not, as one might expect, cause Crow to retreat inward. Instead, Sheryl Crow became even more shrill, angry and more determined than ever to instruct the entire population on how to save itself.

Past generations of celebrities were absorbed by the civil rights movement, a worthy cause. But the current crop of celebutards is so focused on global warming, an issue they approach with all the fervor and drama of a religious cult, it's rapidly becoming farce. In their minds, the planet is being rapidly destroyed, and they have been deputized to save it. As in a post-apocalyptic movie, where the main characters can see into the future—and it's a melted mess—the well-heeled global warming crowd will stop at nothing to force you to give up modern conveniences, paper products and fossil-burning fuels. Just don't ask your fellow celebs to join in the sacrifice. That would be hard.

Sheryl Crow teamed up with like-minded loon Laurie David in April 2007 to attend the White House Correspondents dinner, the annual Washington dinner party/prom. It was, by every account, a toxic combination. At the dinner, the two women, like bloodhounds seizing upon prey, spied President Bush's Deputy Chief of Staff Karl Rove. It soon got ugly.

According to an account posted by the global-warming gals in the *Huffington Post*, Crow and David accosted Rove, and demanded that he "consider taking a fresh look at the science of global warming."

Crow and David tried to lecture Rove that America leads the world in global warming-causing pollution, a dubious charge to say the least. He countered that the United Sates spends more on researching the causes of climate change than any other country. The women were not getting what they wanted, which apparently was nothing less than total agreement. Or maybe blood. The confrontation then took a turn for the bizarre.

Rove apparently said something about China being worse (far worse), and he tried to return to his seat. Crow then touched Rove's arm so he could not escape. "Don't touch me," he said.

"You can't speak to us like that, you work for us," Crow said she answered to this perceived insult.

"I don't work for you, I work for the American people," said Rove, according to Crow and David's account.

Crow insists she got in the last word. "We are the American people!"

But writing in the *National Review Online*, Byron York said an eyewitness's report suggested that Crow and David were "a bit more confrontational than they portrayed themselves in their own account of the incident."

He wrote that immediately after being introduced to Rove by *New York Times* columnist Maureen Dowd, "David began lecturing Rove about global warming. 'This administration has done nothing on the issue,' she told Rove. 'We face a crisis. The time to act is now. This administration has done nothing . . .' "

David, according to this account, told Rove he needed to bring in new people to tell him the "truth" about global warming. When Rove mentioned White House science adviser John Marburger "Crow began poking Rove's chest with her finger, demanding to know what corporations were underwriting Marburger's work." With Crow still jabbing Rove in the chest, he finally started back to his seat. That's when Crow grabbed his arm. She's lucky she didn't get tossed in the street like some crazy stalker.

Rove had little to add about the insane confrontation of which Crow and David are so proud. "She came over to insult me, and she succeeded," was all he would say.

White House spokesman Tony Fratto zinged, "We have respect for the opinions and passion that many people have for climate change. I wish the same respect was afforded to the president."

The next month, Crow announced on her website that she had officially joined the upper strata of the celebustocracy. She'd adopted a two-week-old boy. But how?

Normally, agencies will not adopt out an infant to a woman, particularly a single mother, following such a recent cancer diagnosis. But Sheryl Crow is no ordinary woman. She is a wealthy, internationally famous individual, not to mention a self-appointed planetary savior. The rules appear to be different for her.

For the sake of the child, I pray Sheryl Crow remains well.

9

All the Wrong Moves

TOM CRUISE

☆

Here's the problem. You don't know the history of psychiatry. I do.
—Tom Cruise to *Today* show host Matt Lauer, June 28, 2005

HE SHOT TO FAME dancing in his underwear in 1983's *Risky Business*, and came into his own as an action star in *Mission Impossible*. But then, folks coast-to-coast started questioning his sanity after he jumped on Oprah Winfrey's couch while declaring love for vacant-eyed Katie Holmes. He finally fell to a level of disrepute normally reserved for schoolyard flashers when he slammed Brooke Shields for using prescription medication to quell post-partum depression.

He is Tom Cruise: Scientologist and all-around loon. He's included here not for any earthly political penchant, but for a stunning and complete lack of judgment and disconnection with reality that very nearly rivals a sober Mel Gibson's.

Thomas Cruise Mapother IV was born in Syracuse, New York, on July 3, 1962, to Mary Lee, a special education teacher, and Thomas Cruise Mapother III, an electrical engineer and, Cruise has said, a bully whose last name he dropped at age twelve. Cruise found acting success early and did not attend college. He claims to have suffered as a child from learning disabilities. But like much else in life, he overcame this hardship not with conventional therapy, but with the religion made popular by the Hollywood crowd, Scientology.

At twenty-three he married Mimi Rogers, six years his senior, who introduced him to the faith. The couple split three years later after Cruise refused to perform his husbandly duties. "He was seriously thinking of becoming a monk," Rogers told *Playboy*. "He thought he had to be celibate to maintain the purity of his instrument, but my instrument needed tuning, and we had to split."

His second marriage, to actress Nicole Kidman, started in 1990, the same year he was declared *People* magazine's "Sexiest Man Alive." It lasted ten years and they adopted two children. According to Andrew Morton's book, *Tom Cruise: An Unauthorized Biography*, Kidman, who became a Scientologist, was on the outs after conceding in a 1999 interview: "I was raised Catholic, and a big part of me is still a Catholic girl." She was three months pregnant when she learned about the impending divorce from Cruise's lawyer. She then lost the baby. Tom sent flowers, but did not visit. Only later, Kidman, who stands five feet, ten and a-half inches, was able to joke about her five-foot-seven ex-mate: "At least now I can wear heels."

Over the years, Cruise has sued or threatened to sue at least four individuals and publications for advancing persistent rumors that he is gay, which he vigorously denies. Gay porn actor Chad Slater was ordered to pay Cruise $10 million in damages for telling a celebrity magazine about a purported love affair.

Cruise was foolish to concentrate on rumors that no one really cared about. He should have paid more notice to the day the public turned against him en masse. That happened the moment Cruise fired his long-time publicist, Pat Kingsley, who forbid journalists, at the peril of losing access, to talk about Scientology. Cruise replaced her for a time with his sister, Lee Ann Devette, who had no such qualms. And thus, we met the real Tom Cruise—abrasive, wild-eyed. And mean.

Disaster followed. Cruise was freakishly testy during his interview with Matt Lauer, denying the existence of chemical imbalances, declaring that he alone knew the history of psychiatry. And he slammed Lauer as "glib" for defending Brooke Shields' decision to take medication to conquer the baby blues. Shields called Cruise's words "irresponsible and dangerous." But Tom apologized to Brooke, and the stars made up.

On April 18, 2006, Katie Holmes, sixteen years Tom's junior, gave birth to daughter Suri. During Katie's pregnancy, Cruise raised the collective blood pressure by telling GQ magazine he thought the placenta and umbilical cord would be "very nutritious." He said, "I'm gonna eat the placenta." He later cracked to Diane Sawyer, "Yeah, we're going to do that—a whole family thing. Isn't that normal and natural?" Then he added, "No, we're not eating it."

During Katie's pregnancy, Cruise raised the collective blood pressure by telling GQ magazine he thought the placenta and umbilical cord would be "very nutritious."

Message to Tom: it's not funny if what you say is believable.

Stories were rampant that the birth would be "silent," in keeping with Scientology dictates. Cruise did not deny this entirely. "It's really about respecting the woman," he told GQ. "It's not about her not screaming." He told Sawyer, "The mother makes as much noise . . . you know, she's going through it. But why have other people make noise? You know, you want that area very calm and to make it very special."

As a present for Katie, Cruise didn't buy diamonds (or a muzzle). He bought a home ultrasound machine. Very creepy. Doctors complained that sonograms, which check babies' development, should be performed only by trained technicians. But if Katie had a problem with that or with anything else, absolutely no light was shed on the matter by Diane Sawyer, who had the blank-faced starlet alone in a rare interview for eight-plus minutes in January 2008 on *Good Morning America*. The diva broadcaster talked for five minutes about the Scientology convert's shoes. But not one substantive question crossed her lips about the state of Katie and Tom's weird union.

She also didn't ask about suggestions in Morton's biography that Tom was No. 2 man in his church, or even that Suri was not Cruise's child at all, but was conceived, *Rosemary's Baby*–style, from the frozen sperm of late Scientology founder L. Ron Hubbard. Cruise's lawyer, Bertram Fields, called that and everything else in the book "a pack of lies."

I got an up-close peek at the "hyperactive midlife crisis and sometime actor," as I referred to Cruise, as he took New York—by helicopter, motorcycle, fire truck and rented subway car—in May 2006 to promote *Mission Impossible 3*. What a shock. Cruise over the years had morphed from teen looker, to Arnold Scwarzenegger-wannabe, to attention-starved "Norma Desmond, croaking for his close-up," as I duly noted. He would try to make me pay for that.

From the cheap seats in the press, you see how much control a single, little man can exert on an entire city in the middle of a busy work day in the interest of self-promotion. Arriving on the back of a fire truck, Tom brought traffic to a halt in bustling Times Square. He demanded that I, a lowly columnist, sit through his new movie before being allowed to approach. A publicist told me this rule came down "from the top." The top?

A screening was arranged on that very day. Though the theater was designed to seat 1,000, only one journalist and I attended. Fortunately for Cruise, the movie was pretty good. But then, I'm a sucker for action flicks.

Not so good was the reception we got later, as Tom, looking like a toddler taken off his Ritalin by drug-hating Scientologists, ridiculously played New York City action hero. I was shoved in the chest by a cop and threatened with arrest by a press bunny when I innocently bisected his air space on a public street. Under peril of bodily harm, I did manage to retrieve an autograph for my then-seven-year-old daughter, who remains strangely loyal to Cruise. Well, they *were* the same size. But the actor no doubt regretted signing after he read my column on his wild and wooly day. It led him to personally ban a photographer from the *New York Post* from the Los Angeles premiere *of Mission Impossible 3*. The news was actually encouraging. Tom reads!

> *I did manage to retrieve an autograph for my then-seven-year-old daughter, who remains strangely loyal to Cruise. Well, they were the same size.*

So is Tom Cruise whacked? You decide. I now present Tom—in his own words. Here is a partial transcript of a 2004 videotape produced by the Church of Scientology as a recruitment tool. It's Tom at his most maniacal.

(Not surprisingly, the church succeeded in getting countless copies pulled off the Internet by threatening to take legal action for "copyright infringement." But after Morton's book came out, the folks at gawker.com refused to remove it. They did the sane, movie-going public a tremendous service.)

It starts with an announcer:

"But if that's what Mr. Cruise has brought to this world, there still remains one more word on the man. Call it: Tom Cruise on Tom Cruise, Scientologist.

Music that sounds like the distorted theme music from *Mission: Impossible* plays in the background. Tom punctuates his words with karate chops and "whoops."

Here he is:

"I think it's a privilege to call yourself a Scientologist and it's something you have to earn. And because a Scientologist does, he or she has the ability to create new and better realities, and improve conditions. Uh, being a Scientologist, you look at someone and you know absolutely that you can help them.

"There's a time I went through this and I said, 'You know what?' When I read it ah, you know, I just went phooo. This is it; is exactly it.

"Being a Scientologist, when you drive past an accident, it's not like anyone else, it's, you drive past, you know you have to do something about it. You know you are the only one who can really help.

"But that's . . . that's what drives me is that I know that we have an opportunity and, uh, to really help for the first time and effectively change people's lives, and ah I'm dedicated to that. I'm gonna, I'm absolutely, uncompromisingly dedicated to that.

"Orgs [Scientology organizations] are there to help, OK. But we, also as the public, we have a responsibility. It's not just the orgs. It's not just [church leader] Dave Miscavige. You know, it's not just not just me. It's you. It's everyone out there kinda rereading KSW ["Keep Scientology working"] and looking what needs to be done and saying, okay, am I gonna do it or am I not gonna do it? Period. And am I gonna look at that guy or am I too afraid because I have my own out-ethics [ethics are tools needed to apply the principles of Scientology; out-ethics go against Scientology] to put in someone else's ethics? And that's all it comes down to . . .

"We are the authorities on getting people off drugs. We are the authorities on the mind. We are the authorities on improving conditions. Crimanon [a program that treats criminals]. We can rehabilitate criminals. We can bring peace and unite cultures. That once you know these tools and you know that they work, it's not good enough that I'm just doing okay.

"Traveling the world and meeting the people that I've met, you know, talking with these leaders in various fields, [pause] they want help, and they are depending on people who know and who can be effective, and do it, and that's us. That is our responsibility

to do that. It is the time now. Now is the time. It is being a Scientologist, people are turning to you, and you better know it, and if you
don't, you know, go and learn it. [Laughs] but don't pretend you
know it, or whatever.

"It's like, we're here to help. If you're a Scientologist, you see
life, things, the way they are, in all it's glory, in all of its complex-
ity, and the more you know as a Scientologist, the more you become overwhelmed by it. [Laughs again, clapping hands]

"I wish the world was a different place, I'd like to go on vacation, play, and just do that. Know what I mean? I mean that's how I
want it to be. There's times I'd like to do that, but I can't because I
know, I know, so, you know, I have to do something about it . . . It's
not . . .

"You can just see the look in their eyes. You know the ones
who are doing it, and you know the spectators [dabblers in Scientology, the worst], the ones who are going, 'Well, it's easy for you.
That thing, I've canceled that in my area.

"[Laughs] It's like, man, you're either in or you're out. That
spectatorism, I've no time for it. That is something we have no
time for now.

"So it's our responsibility to educate, create the new reality. We
have that responsibility to say, hey, this is the way it should be
done. We do it this way and people are actually getting better. Let's
get it done. Let's get it really done.

"Have enough love, compassion and toughness, that you're
going to do it, and do it right."

Announcer: "A Scientologist can be defined by a single question: 'Would you want others to achieve the knowledge you now
have?' In answering that question, Tom Cruise has introduced LRH
[L. Ron Hubbard] technology to over one billion people of Earth,
and that's only the first wave he's unleashed, which is why the story
of Tom Cruise, Scientologist, has only just begun."

In another video to emerge, Tom Cruise takes credit for saving the lives of hundreds of poisoned workers at the World Trade Center site, and calls federal officials "liars."

He saves workers. Unites world cultures. Rehabilitates criminals, performs sonograms. And the one billion people on Earth he's reached are just the start.

Next: Tom walks on water. Or is there water in outer space?

10

Crapping Out, One Baby at a Time
BRANGELINA

☆

It's his blood. It's in a . . . I think it's supposed to be for pressed flowers.

> —Angelina Jolie displays a charm containing Billy Bob Thornton's blood to Larry King, August 4, 2001

I think we'll crap out somewhere between seven and nine.

> —Brad Pitt tells Charlie Rose the number of children he wants to produce with Angelina, December 17, 2007

THEY GO TOGETHER, like Hollywood and glamour. Like tattoos and body piercings. Like celebutards and their self-appointed mission to save the planet. They are Angelina Jolie, the bisexual, blood-obsessed, brother-kissing, Illustrated Woman who could badly use a sandwich, and Brad Pitt, the somewhat dim, Angelina-obsessed hunk who could badly use a shave.

Without the benefit of marriage, they have adopted children from around the world, and birthed one of their own in a Namibian clinic and two more in France. Despite demanding film careers and a globe-trotting life-style—their kids have attended more schools in a single year than some of us have seen in a lifetime—this strange and golden couple, collectively known in the press as "Brangelina," has found time to do high-profile humanitarian work, Brad for victims of Hurricane Katrina and Angie for the United Nations High Commissioner for Refugees. However well-meaning her volunteerism, Angelina Jolie has failed to address the extreme controversies that have shamed other UN efforts, specifically the Oil for Food scandal and allegations that women were raped by UN peacekeeping troops in Congo. And no interviewer, not even Anderson Cooper, who had Angelina all to himself for a couple of hours, has pressed her to speak out about such unpleasant things.

William Bradley Pitt was born December 18, 1963, in Shawnee, Oklahoma, and raised in Springfield, Missouri, the son of Jane Etta, a high school counselor, and William Alvin Pitt, a truck company owner. Angelina Jolie Voight, as she was known at birth, followed Brad into the world nearly a dozen years later, on June 4, 1975, in Los Angeles, California, the daughter of actors Jon Voight and Marcheline Bertrand. Bertrand, who died from ovarian cancer in 2007, was French Canadian, Voight German and Slovak. Her parents split up a year after her birth, and Marcheline gave up acting to raise Angelina and her older brother. Angelina's relationship with Dad has always been fraught. Now she won't speak to him.

Brad's background was the more conventional. He attended the University of Missouri, majoring in journalism, but left two credits short of graduating to move to California, initially supporting himself by driving strippers in limousines, moving refrigerators, and dressing up as a giant chicken for the restaurant chain el Pollo Loco. He got noticed, big-time, in a supporting role as a hustler in 1991's *Thelma and Louise* in which he took off his shirt, donned a cowboy hat, and worked his way into the fantasies of millions of women and more than a few men. Like his buddy and *Oceans Eleven*, *Twelve* and *Thirteen* co-star George Clooney, he's twice been named *People* magazine's Sexiest Man Alive. In 2000, he married *Friends* TV star Jennifer Aniston, a marriage that, for years, seemed like the rare Hollywood keeper. That is, until he met Angelina Jolie.

Angie, as she's called, was a self-described "drama queen" who, as a child in Palisades, New York, wore glasses and braces, and failed as an early model. She complained that she looked like a Muppet, all skinny and goofy. As a self-loathing teen, she started cutting herself. She lived with a boyfriend, and as Jolie boasted in too-much-information interviews, the pair was heavily involved in sado-masochistic sexual activity. She was so obsessed with death, she fantasized about becoming a funeral director, but instead attended acting classes and majored in film at New York University before dropping out to act.

In 1995, while filming the movie *Hackers*, she met her first husband, Jonny Lee Miller. She said about him, "You're young, you're drunk, you're in bed, you have knives; sh*t happens." How romantic. She wore black leather pants to her wedding and a white shirt with Miller's name written across the back in her blood. No surprise the marriage was doomed.

After starring with Jenny Shimizu in *Foxfire* in 1996, the pair were said to have an openly lesbian relationship. Jolie told *Elle* magazine, "When I was twenty, I fell in love with somebody who happened to be a woman." Asked by Barbara Walters if she was bisexual, she said, "Of course. If I fell in love with a woman tomorrow, would I feel that it's okay to want to kiss and touch her? If I fell in love with her? Absolutely! Yes!" Only much later, ensconced with Brad Pitt, Jolie had second thoughts. "I've never hidden my bisexuality, but since I've been with Brad, there's no longer a place for that or S&M in my life." Shimizu didn't buy it. Lesbianism is "like a drug and she was hooked," she told the United Kingdom's *News of the World* in 2007.

Jolie hit the big time in 2000, accepting the Best Supporting Actress Oscar for her convincing portrayal of mental patient Lisa Rowe in the 1999 film, *Girl, Interrupted*. In the audience, she was seen manically tongue-kissing and caressing her older brother, James Haven. Ew.

"I'm so in love with my brother right now," she said while thanking the academy. Even in Hollywood, this attracted attention. The pair, by the way, have denied having an incestuous relationship.

Jolie engaged in one more starter marriage, wedding actor and director Billy Bob Thornton in 2000. He was forty-four. She was twenty-four. The

"I'm so in love with my brother right now," she said while thanking the academy. Even in Hollywood, this attracted attention.

pair wore each other's blood around their necks so they might remain close when filming in remote locations. Apparently, they were unaware that cellphones were a more sanitary option. I've seen them on TV, making out so fervently, it was enough to make one ill. They adopted Angie's first child, a son named Maddox, in Cambodia, just months before divorcing in 2002.

That year, Jolie's sometimes estranged father, Jon Voight, went to the celebrities' favorite counseling center, *Access Hollywood*, to declare that his daughter had "serious emotional problems." Angie dropped the name "Voight" legally from her moniker. She said, "My father and I don't speak . . . I don't believe that somebody's family becomes their blood. Because my son's adopted, families are earned."

Her tattoos are the stuff of Hollywood legend and Middle-American ridicule. Space prohibits me from naming all her body illustrations, but they include: A lower case "h" inside her left wrist in honor of her brother, James Haven, and also for Timothy Hutton, whom she once dated. (After they broke up, she said it was only for James.) A quotation from Tennessee Williams on her left forearm. The global coordinates representing the birthplaces of her first four children on her left arm, covering an earlier "Bill Bob" tattoo. An Asian tiger on her back. The saying, "that which nourishes me also destroys me." And an "M" on the palm of her hand for her late mother, Marcheline. She was so covered in tattoos, it was joked at the 2007 funeral of murdered "Realtor to the Stars" Linda Stein that the woman bullied Angie into concealing her ink while applying to snooty Manhattan co-op boards for apartments.

During the filming of 2005's *Mr. and Mrs. Smith*, Angie met Brad. Evidently, the couple's on-screen chemistry was matched by the fireworks off-screen. But Jolie denied that she engaged in a sexual relationship with Pitt until he'd split from Jennifer Aniston, telling Britain's *Grazia* magazine that sleeping with another woman's husband is "one of the worst things you can do."

"He was married to his best friend who he loves and respects," she said.

She told an interviewer, "To be intimate with a married man, when my own father cheated on my mother, is not something I could forgive. I could not look at myself in the morning if I did that. I wouldn't be attracted to a man who would cheat on his wife."

Conventional wisdom had it that Jennifer lost Brad partly because she did not want his children, which she denies. It did not help Brad's image in the eyes of his "best friend" when pictures surfaced of Brad and Angie together in Africa with son Maddox while Brad was still married to Aniston. "The world was shocked and I was shocked," she told *Vanity Fair*.

Pitt proceeded to pose with Jolie in a photo shoot he helped devise for *W* magazine, in which the pair is done up like a 1963 couple and posed with a passel of children at the dinner table. Brad said he wanted to explore the "unidentifiable malaise" that can haunt a seemingly happy couple. "You don't know what's wrong, because the marriage is everything you signed up for."

Aniston retorted that the exercise proved, "there's a sensitivity chip that's missing," in Brad.

Brad and Angie set out to create a village. In 2005, an Ethiopian baby, Zahara, joined Maddox, whose initial father, Billy Bob, had dropped out of the picture.

In May 2006, Jolie gave birth to Brad's daughter, Shiloh Nouvel Jolie-Pitt, in Namibia, Africa, by a scheduled Caesarean section. And in March 2007, Jolie adopted a three-year-old Vietnamese boy, Pax Thien Jolie-Pitt. Brad has lent his surname to all the children. Yet while the countries from which the Jolie-Pitts obtain their progeny willingly hand the kids to Angie, they refuse to grant adoptions to a man, not her husband, for fear of boosting child trafficking. And still, the family has had little trouble growing. This has led to considerable criticism of Angie and Brad. Isn't there room in their lives to save American-born orphans?

Angie slammed her sister in international adoption, Madonna, after the singer drew international outrage by taking home African non-orphan David Banda. "Personally, I prefer to stay on the right side of the law," Angie sniffed. "I would never take a child away from a place where adoption is illegal." But later, she backtracked, saying that she was "horrified" by the attacks on the singer.

Jolie got a small taste of what can happen when you're not careful to ensure that the child you save is really motherless, when the supposed Ethiopian birth mother of little Zahara emerged in the press, claiming the child was the product of rape. But the woman backed off of her claim to the baby. She said she was glad Zahara was being raised by such a fabulous couple.

To thank Anderson Cooper of CNN for his reports about African refugees, Angelina sat for a two-hour interview in 2006 that the network hoped would capitalize on the birth of her daughter. Angelina hoped the chat would help her pet cause. To Cooper, she revealed that she donated one-third of her "stupid" income to help save the world, and intended to have even more children. She also demonstrated incredible naivety about the institutions she supports. Cooper prodded her with kid gloves about the United Nations Oil for Food scandal, in which UN officials and enemies of our country conspired to piggishly enrich themselves by looting a program created to exchange Iraqi oil for food and medicine. He never mentioned rape accusations against UN peacekeepers in Congo. He did gently mention the UN's criminally slow response to the genocide in Rwanda.

Jolie jumped to the defense of the United Nations.

"I think we hear a lot of—we certainly hear a lot of the negative things and—about the UN. You know, you hear—you hear about the negative things that have gone on. You don't hear on a daily basis the amount of people that are kept alive or protected by the UN. And if that list was plastered everywhere, I think people would be in shock and have a little more respect. I certainly think it needs to—it needs reform. I mean, it's certainly not a perfect organization, by any means. It's the closest thing that we have got, you know, to—to a real international institution that listens to all sides, represents all sides, and—and can make a certain—certain kinds of decisions. . . .

"I have gone to countries where I have wanted to be angry about something. And you realize there's such a fine balance, because you also have to be—they have to be allowed to work in these countries."

She was on fire, but she had no solutions. "And you just, God, feel—feel like, you know, how—how many times are we going to let these things go on this long? Or when are we going to finally be united internationally to be able to handle these things immediately and . . ." she said about the genocide in Darfur.

Cooper asked no follow up questions.

On December 5, 2007, Brad Pitt took a turn with Larry King, in which the broadcaster interviewed him in New Orleans, where he was building houses. As always, the conversation turned to family. But Larry, in his fashion, was not nearly as credulous as Anderson Cooper. The interview soon resembled comedy.

KING: One other thing about your kids. How did you bang, bang? Maddox, Zahara, Pax and Shiloh—that is not Jane/Mary.

PITT: No. We—I can't—I can't tell you anything more than it just felt right. And . . . Yes. It just kind of—we stumbled on it and after much deliberation and—when it felt right, it felt right. I can't explain it.

KING: Do you want more children?

BRAD: Oh, yes. Yes. Yes. . . . We're just getting started.

KING: Four and you're just getting started?

PITT: We'll see. We'll, you know, we'll probably crap out somewhere. I don't know. But, yes, we're not done.

KING: Doesn't it hit a point where there's too many?

Lest you think the Bradster misspoke, the comedy kept on coming a couple of weeks later, when he spoke to Charlie Rose.

"I think we'll crap out somewhere between seven and nine children," he said. "Yeah, somewhere in there, we'll crap out."

In 2008, it happened again. Jolie gave birth to Brad's twins, Vivienne Marcheline and Knox Léon. Brangelina were paid $14 million by *People* magazine for the happy, grinning faces of the twins. *New York* magazine speculated that the pictures were Photoshopped after *Parenting* magazine reported that babies less than two to three months old "do not smile from exterior stimulation." The couple planned to marry, finally, in New Orleans.

Six kids down. One or two to go. The crap out point is drawing near.

11

Bowling for Cheeseburgers
MICHAEL MOORE

Thank God for the Canadians. They're just like us—only better!

—Michael Moore at the Democratic National Convention,
July 27, 2004

MICHAEL MOORE WILL NOT be ignored.

The puffy pontificator and Oscar-winning filmmaker masquerades as a congenial, harmless nebbish. But at the core of his propaganda is a deep-seated disdain for all things American, and he will fudge facts or outright lie to get this message across. Madonna and the rest of the Hollywood crowd are so smitten with Moore, he might be considered the guru of the far left. But take everything he says with a grain of salt. Better yet, ignore it altogether. If you can.

Michael Francis Moore was born April 23, 1954, in Flint, Michigan, the son of Veronica, a secretary, and Frank Moore, an auto assembly-line worker. He's married to producer Kathleen Glynn, and lives in New York, where he claims to be a practicing Roman Catholic. Fun-fact: After winning a tournament as a youth, Moore was named a lifetime member of the National Rifle Association. He would later address his dislike for guns in *Bowling for Columbine*.

It comes as little surprise that Moore dropped out of the University of Michigan-Flint—a trend of the celebutard set. He was named the editor of *Mother Jones* magazine in California for a mere four months in 1986, before he was fired for refusing to print an article that criticized the Sandinistas' human-rights record in Nicaragua. Mind you, this was not because he doubted the article's premise. Rather, Moore feared that President Ronald Reagan might say, "See, even *Mother Jones* agrees with me."

The article's author, Paul Berman, summed up Moore perfectly as a "very ideological guy and not a very well-educated guy." The kind of warped reasoning that made Moore kill the article—damn the truth for politics!—would color the rest of his career, and even feed his first commercial success: He won $58,000 in a settlement over wrongful termination from the magazine. He used this money to help make the film *Roger and Me*. A monster was born.

Released in 1989, *Roger and Me* is a documentary about the effects of closing General Motors auto plants in Flint, Michigan—with a heavy subtext of corporation-bashing. The movie was humorous and gripping. And completely misleading. It set the tone for everything to come.

In the movie, Moore changed the chronological order of events for shock value. He shows a family being evicted from their home at the moment the chairman of General Motors, Roger Smith, gives a Christmas message. In reality, the two events did not coincide. He also shows President Ronald Reagan visiting Flint as the town collapses. In truth, the footage was shot years earlier, in 1979, when Reagan was merely a candidate for high office, not president.

The film is based on the premise that Moore tried, repeatedly and unsuccessfully, to interview chairman Smith, who manages to hide from him. Yet this is belied by unearthed footage that shows Moore questioning Smith during a 1987 General Motors shareholders meeting. That session is not in the film.

Overall, film critic Pauline Kael slammed the movie for exaggerating the impact of the plant's closing on the community. It didn't matter. At the time of release *Roger and Me* was the most successful documentary in American history. It's since been surpassed at the box office by Moore's *Bowling for Columbine* and *Fahrenheit 911*.

Out in 2002, *Bowling for Columbine* is another political screed using documentary techniques, this one about gun ownership in America. It was so preachy and over-the-top, the movie very nearly made me run out and buy an Uzi. And I favor gun control.

The premise is that Canada, Moore's utopia to the north, has a much lower rate of gun violence, despite similar levels of gun ownership as the United States—a completely disingenuous claim that Moore uses to condemn the violent American culture. But Moore knows very well that the ownership of handguns is far lower in Canada than in the States. Still, this fact does not stop him from making fun of hunters who, in the scheme of things, are not a major part of the problem.

But the moment in the film that had me running for the gun cabinet came when Moore interviewed then National Rifle Association president Charlton Heston. As soon as the men sat down, Moore began hectoring the gun enthusiast about his support for firearms. Heston had no choice but to walk away from the chat, as the camera rolled. Even so, Moore theatrically placed a photograph of a six-year-old school shooting victim, Kayla Rolland, at Heston's feet. Was he suggesting Heston was a murderer? Please! The arrogance.

Bowling for Columbine won an Academy Award for Best Documentary Feature. When he picked up his award, Moore couldn't contain himself. He said, onstage, to boos and cheers: "We like nonfiction and we live in fictitious times. We live in a time where we have fictitious election results, that elect a fictitious president. We live in a time where we have a man sending us to war for fictitious reasons."

Oscar host Steve Martin couldn't help himself either, cracking, "The Teamsters are helping Mr. Moore into the trunk of his limo."

I confess that, being weak of stomach, I did not sit through the entirety of *Fahrenheit 911*. I fundamentally object to films that commandeer the tragedy of September 11, 2001, in a cynical effort to advance a political agenda. And from what I've seen, Moore does this shamelessly, examining ties between the United States government and Saudi Arabia, particularly the family of Osama bin Laden. This point of view may be fodder for a very good film. Not a disjointed, sputtering, political rant by Michael Moore.

> *Oscar host Steve Martin couldn't help himself either, cracking, "The Teamsters are helping Mr. Moore into the trunk of his limo."*

And yet, *Fahrenheit 911* is the most successful documentary of all time. It didn't get an Oscar, though. Moore did not enter it as Best Documentary, trying instead for a Best Picture award. It did not even get nominated. Pity.

I caught up with Michael Moore during the 2004 Democratic convention, where he hung out with like-minded celebutard Jimmy Carter, and was treated as a hero. While the convention was held in Boston, the nearby college town of Cambridge, Massachusetts had been taken over by hard-core leftists. People such as ex-presidential candidate, screaming Howard Dean, who laughed at his own crack, "You can't call the president a fascist—we're not trying to do that this week, anyway!" He was perfect company for Moore, who appeared goofy, jumpy and giggly.

"Thank God for the Canadians," he crowed to an audience. "They're just like us, only better. They just wish we would read a little more."

I wanted to ask, "So when are you going, eh?"

In the 2007 film *Sicko*, Moore blasts America's certainly imperfect health care system, while lionizing those in Europe and even Cuba. I'll tell you about a piece I saw on CNN, normally no stranger to far-left politics. In this one, though, Dr. Sanjay Gupta had both guns blazing as he interviewed Moore about the movie.

"People will walk away with the perception that health care is free in England and Canada. . . ." Gupta said as Moore interrupted.

"It is free! It is free! It is free!" he insisted.

But Gupta interjected with the obvious, "You pay for it through taxes." And he rattled off the high tax rates in France, where "free" health care rips a sizable chunk from the family income.

Moore sat there, speechless, shaking his head. He had no answer.

"We've got Michael Moore speechless," said Gupta. "That's pretty hard to do."

It's hard to stump Michael Moore when he's surrounded by his regular cheering section. Alone, he is a fool.

I wonder—if no one listened to Michael Moore, would he cease to exist?

12

Desperately Seeking Sanity
MADONNA

Dr. King, Malcolm X, freedom of speech is as good as sex.
And if you don't vote, you're going to get a spankie.
>   —Madonna, in bra and combat boots, rapping in a public
>   service video, 1990

I'm coming from a point of view now, from experience,
so I can help people, share what I know. I think of every-
thing I do, 'How is this going to affect other people?
What will they get out of this? Am I adding to the chaos
of the world? Am I part of the problem, or the solution?'
>   —Madonna, in top hat, to *Harpers & Queen*, November 2005

MADONNA. THE MATERIAL GIRL. The Material Mom. Madge.
Mrs. Ritchie. Slut. Whatever you call her, it cannot be denied that
few in history have accomplished so much—she's catapulted into
an international cottage industry through movies, music, books,
and her own naked body—with so very little. Her rise to the title of
world's top-earning female performer is impressive. Less so is her
head-scratching ability to convince audiences that she has some-

thing terribly important to say about politics, religion or world affairs, simply because this sexual savant can afford the biggest toys.

Madonna sprang onto the scene in the early 1980s, wriggling her sweetly pudgy form in Spandex and a crucifix, and has shaped herself into arguably the world's most famous woman, raking in an estimated $325 million. Over the decades she's evolved from an ambitious gal who acted out, ad nauseam, against her own sexual hang ups and perceived repression, to one who leaped into the body of a sinewy, tweed-wearing, British-accented stick-in-the mud obsessed with the Jewish mystical religion, Kabbalah.

Along the way, Madonna has undergone many earth-shaking personal reinventions designed to keep her in the public eye. She was a free spirit in her early film, *Desperately Seeking Susan*, a breathy bombshell playing opposite Warren Beatty in *Dick Tracy*, and a weirdly prudish hussy done up, nude and self-conscious, in bondage gear in her coffee table book, *Sex*. In her 1991 documentary, *Truth or Dare*, Madonna graciously admitted she was neither the world's greatest singer nor dancer. And still, she became a bigger star than the world has seen.

Her props of choice are relics of her Roman Catholic faith, chiefly crucifixes and rosaries that she employs as sex toys. A 1989 video for "Like a Prayer," featured stigmata and Madonna making out with Jesus. It lost the artist an endorsement deal with Pepsi, and brought down a rain of condemnation from defenders of the Catholic church. Which may have been the entire point. For a while, she held the power to make one wonder how far she'd go to shock.

Madonna Louise Ciccone—a second middle name, Veronica, was added unofficially at her confirmation—was born August 16, 1958, in Bay City, Michigan, the third of six children born to an Italian-American father, Silvio "Tony" Ciccone, and a mother of French-Canadian descent, Madonna Louise Fortin.

Madonna would be haunted for much of her life by the death of her namesake mother from breast cancer when she was just five years old. Her lack of a female nurturer is a theme that crops up, over and over, in her work. In interviews and song lyrics, she points to a strict, and possibly abusive, relationship with her father.

Later, Tony Ciccone married the family housekeeper, and had two more children.

Madonna attended the University of Michigan, dropping out after her sophomore year to pursue a dance career in New York City, arriving in town with just $35.00 in her pocket. She worked at Dunkin' Donuts, and as a nude model. In 1982, she signed her first record deal. She was on her way.

In 1985, she married the actor Sean Penn, forming a disastrous union that dissolved into allegations of domestic violence (by Penn). Many other affairs ensued, but they always took a back seat to her career, which seemed to know no ceiling. It all climaxed, if you will, with Madonna's coffee table book, *Sex*, and the album, *Erotica*, which at the time looked to be the biggest controversy of her life. She had no idea.

Sex, a volume hidden behind Mylar wrap and covered in weighty metal, retailed for $49.95, an exorbitant sum when you consider that ordinary pornography such as *Penthouse* or *Hustler* sold for less than one-tenth the price, and could be read with one hand. But *Sex* was promoted as an art book. It featured black-and-white photographs of a nude Madonna in all manner of poses, from bondage to something akin to prostitution. However, the images struck me as posed and decidedly unsexy and not very artful.

Madonna insisted earnestly that she rebelled against society's sexual repression, a weight she said all women are forced to live under. It made me wonder—what the hell is she talking about?

By 1992, American women had the ability to take lovers and careers without repercussions. Madonna herself was proof of that. Also, AIDS had put a damper on sexual acting out. The repression she complained of in *Sex* seemed a personal problem best discussed with a trained therapist. *Sex* is now in demand as a relic of the era, but it did not do so well at the time.

Madonna had accomplished everything she'd set out to do, and more. At 38, she starred in *Evita*, playing Argentina's first lady, Eva Peron, who died when she was but thirty-three. Then, four days before her forty-second birthday, in August 2000, Madonna gave birth to her second child, Rocco John Ritchie. She married his dad, British filmmaker Guy Ritchie, ten years her junior, later that year. Rocco joined a household that included daughter Lourdes, born out of wedlock to Madonna in 1996.

But for a standard celebutard, the bigger the star, the more compelled she is to align herself with the leftist cause du jour. Onstage at her top-grossing *Confessions* tour, she made obscene comments about President George W. Bush. At Madison Square Garden, she instructed fans to go out and see the film, *Fahrenheit 911*, in which her rotund celebrity pal, Michael Moore, blasts the administration's war on terror in Afghanistan and Iraq.

"I don't think I've ever cried so hard at a movie in my life," Madonna said.

As she rounded the bend toward fifty, she'd lost the ability to shock. That didn't stop her. Neither did bombing in a remake of the film, *Swept Away*, directed by her husband.

But Madonna still had one dramatic transformation left, and this renovation may prove her most remarkable of all. She was no longer tongue-kissing babes half her age, or rushing to remove her clothes. Rather, she was in a hurry to put them on. She wrote children's books, none featuring pictures you'd ban from the kids' bedroom. And most strangely, the woman from Michigan developed a fake English accent. She'd come a long way from her spankie days. Madonna was reborn once again. She turned into a middle-aged mom. Madonna gave a fawning interview to Britain's *Harpers & Queen* in 2005, in which she revealed that she can be a tyrant to Lourdes, or "Lola." Lourdes was barely nine years old at the time, and sharing a home with Rocco, the child of Madonna and step dad Guy Ritchie. Her own father, personal trainer Carlos Leon, was cast out of Madonna's life shortly after she was born. It is unclear how much of a role Madonna allows Carlos to have in his little girl's life, since his name never came up.

"I'm the disciplinarian, Guy's the spoiler," Madonna told the magazine. "When Daddy gets home, they're going to get chocolate." Evidently, not milk chocolate, as Madonna insists "We're a TV and dairy-free house." Whole grains, fish and vegetables are in. Ice cream and chocolate milk are definitely out at the Ritchie abode.

"TV is trash. I was raised without it. I didn't miss anything," she also said. "TV is poison. No one even talks about it around here. We don't have magazines or newspapers in the house either." This is the same gal who made a spectacle of herself, on TV, at the 2003 MTV Music Video Awards by sucking face with Britney Spears and Christina Aguilera. In the audience, watching approvingly, were Guy and Lourdes, who was then six, and done up in a white communion dress, lace gloves and a studded belt with the inscription, "Boy Toy." Madonna used to wear that male-bashing slogan around her own waist, long before Lourdes was even conceived. This tacky display was much commented on, but at least, for Madonna's sake, Guy and Lourdes were able to watch Mom's performance, in all its exhibitionistic, sapphic delight, live at Radio City Music Hall—and not on that poisonous TV.

To *Harpers & Queen*, Madonna said that when her children misbehave, "I take privileges away. The kids get to watch movies every Sunday, so if they're naughty they get their movie taken away. They have to be particularly naughty for that one. If they're just a little naughty, then no stories before bed." But Lourdes was subject to the harshest treatment of all. When she fails to pick up her clothes from the bedroom floor, "We take all of her clothes and put them in a bin bag, and they get stuck somewhere, and she has to earn all of her clothes back by being tidy, picking things up in her room, making her bed in the morning, hanging up her clothes, stuff like that." And if the kid staged a tantrum over which outfit to wear, "We have got down to one outfit," said her mom. "She wears the same outfit every day to school until she learns her lesson." Nine years old.

The woman who despises TV will also make an exception if it's her own show, and it includes heavy doses of Kabbalah. "My ultimate goal is to have a TV series, and each episode would be about girls finding themselves in challenging situations."

Madonna, the avid environmentalist featured on the cover of *Vanity Fair*'s "green" issue, raised an international stink in 2006, when she imported at least 1,000 pheasants to her British estate, Ashcombe House, so the birds might be shot to death. Each year, bankers, businessmen and celebrities including Brad Pitt paid more than $19,000 a day to partake in the fancy pheasant hunt. One would think this was beyond hypocritical that Madonna, purported lover of all living things, found herself standing between our feathered friends and being a member of the landed gentry. The hunt was discontinued only after Stella McCartney, designer daughter of Sir Paul, protested, proving that Madonna is nothing if not savvy about to whom she should suck up.

> *Madonna, the avid environmentalist featured on the cover of Vanity Fair's "green" issue, raised an international stink in 2006, when she imported at least 1,000 unfortunate pheasants to her British estate, Ashcombe House, so the birds might be shot to death.*

MADONNA TRIED, and failed, to conceive a second child with Ritchie. Natural motherhood off the table, Madonna, in gold-plated celebutard style, decided to take drastic action. She followed a trail blazed by the likes of Mia Farrow and Angelina Jolie, and turned to a path of self-reinvention that topped nearly everything that came before: she acquired a live toddler from the Third World.

It was October 2006. Fresh from the pheasant hunt, stories

swirled out of Malawi, Africa, that Madonna planned to adopt a local child. It was said that she'd arranged to have twelve boys plucked from orphanages for her to choose from. That troubling image—with its overtones of picking a china pattern to go with the silver, or worse, lining up human beings for a latter-day slave auction—were largely confirmed later on. Madonna told Oprah Winfrey on her nationally televised TV show that she'd put together a list of alternates if her adoption "hadn't worked out".

But for the first few days that Madonna was in Africa, her loyal publicist and serial liar, Liz Rosenberg, vehemently denied that she was in the market for a baby. This kept the press at bay. For a while. Of course, when the story turned out to be true, the knives were gleaming.

In reality, Madonna had her eye on David Banda, a bright-eyed thirteen-month-old who had no idea that his absorption by one of the world's richest women would unleash the furies. Heck, I called Madonna a "sluttish, egomaniacal mother-of the-century" who'd "traveled far beyond her bra-baring, intercourse-simulating, public girl-kissing, Jesus-emulating loser antics to grab attention—and flesh." Phew. I was getting warmed up.

You see, David was no AIDS orphan. He was not even an orphan. In fact, Madonna later admitted to Oprah that he'd been tested for HIV in Africa, and found to be negative. Would she have taken him any other way?

David's adoption created an international uproar when it was revealed he had a biological father. His mother died shortly after his birth, and the family was too poor to provide adequate nourishment for the baby, who would have survived on breast milk. So the father, Yohane Banda, gave him to an orphanage. He said in interviews he didn't realize that handing David to Madonna meant that he'd be giving his child "for good."

In lieu of payment for the baby, Madonna pledged to raise $3 million for orphans through the creation of a center that would preach her pet religion, Kabbalah. Why, I wondered, did Madonna not simply pledge some of that money to help reunite David with his real family?

Local authorities started legal action to block the adoption, but Madonna swept David home to London, where he arrived at the airport in the arms of a nanny. For Madonna, it was now time for image repair.

For this, Madonna put herself in the loving clutches of Oprah Winfrey. Oprah presented her, via satellite, in full floral getup, on her television show.

Madonna went unchallenged when she told her hostess, "I wanted to go into a Third World country, I wasn't sure where, and give a life to a child who otherwise might not have one."

Rather than ask tough questions, Oprah burbled, embarrassingly, "and I say, God bless you for that!" and "Bravo!"

As the clock wound down, an approving Oprah heard Madonna condescend sickeningly toward David's father, calling Yohane Banda "a simple man who comes from a village who has nothing." Better the kid be raised by a mega-wealthy woman who can buy anybody.

She described a court hearing in which Banda, "looked into my eyes and said to me he was grateful I was going to give his son a life and, had he kept him in the village, he would have buried him.

"I didn't need any more confirmation that I was doing the right thing and I had his blessing," she said, telling how the dad signed away the child. Oprah failed to mention that the man could not read.

In 2007, Madonna left Warner Records and signed a $120 million deal with concert promoters Live Nation. But before she could walk, the company made sure to tell the world that Madonna, who still owed the label an album, might as well let the door hit her on the butt.

Warner released a report penned by Bank of America securities analysts with the eye-catching title, "For $120 Million, She's All Yours." The report concluded there is "headline risk associated with a Madonna defection. However, the bigger risk would be to overpay for an artist that does not seem to be generating the revenue to support the contract being discussed." It also pointed out that Madonna will turn sixty years old in the last year of her Live Nation contract.

The deal is "fantastic" for her but does not "make economic sense".

"Her loss will not meaningfully impact Warner's near-term sales."

One word: Ouch.

Surprising no one, in October 2008 Madonna and Guy Ritchie announced they were splitting up, leaving in their imploding union's wake the dregs of Ritchie's unsuccessful directing career and rumors of Madonna's red-hot Kabbalah-fueled love affair with Yankees slugger Alex Rodrigeuz.

13

I'm Not Anti-Semitic; I Just Hate Jews
JIMMY CARTER

It is imperative that the general Arab community and all significant Palestinian groups make it clear that they will end the suicide bombings and other acts of terrorism when international laws and the ultimate goals of the road map for peace are accepted by Israel.

—This passage appeared on page 213 of Jimmy Carter's book, *Palestine: Peace Not Apartheid*, Simon & Schuster 2006

That was a terribly worded sentence which implied, obviously in a ridiculous way, that I approved terrorism and terrorist acts against Israeli citizens.

—Carter, on that passage

HE'S BEEN CALLED a liar. He's been called a bigot. He's been called senile, an anti-Semite and even a plagiarist. Aside from the obvious—the man is clearly a liar, a bigot and an anti-Semite—I wish we could blame what ails Jimmy Carter on senility or laziness. The fact is, he knows exactly what he is doing. The one-term president of the United States has crawled out of the dumpster of irrelevancy

to reinvent himself as a pretend intellectual fond of writing and ut-
tering the most vicious, false and racist screeds imaginable, and he
does so with a smile. At least now people are talking about Jimmy
Carter, the most dangerous ex-world leader alive.

James Earl Carter Jr. was born October 1, 1924 in Plains, Georgia, to Earl Carter, a well-to-do farmer, and Lillian, a nurse. Jimmy,
as Carter's long been known, was the first United States president
born in a hospital. Modern technology didn't help him too much,
though. He attended Georgia Tech and Jackson State University before receiving a Bachelor's of Science degree at the United States
Naval Academy, serving as a submariner in the Atlantic and Pacific
fleets. Carter, who is fond of saying that "Jesus Christ is the driving
force" in his life, then set about a career in politics.

He was governor of Georgia when Richard M. Nixon resigned
the presidency of the United States in 1974. It was an opportunity
he could not resist. Carter was nationally unknown when he sold
himself to the American people as a Beltway outsider and defeated
then-President Gerald Ford in the 1976 presidential election. The
next four years, by most accounts, were a series of disasters interrupted by calamities.

Before he took the oath of office Carter distinguished himself
by becoming the first president to speak to *Playboy* magazine, in
November 1976. He further distinguished himself by issuing an
odd, "adultery-in-my-heart" sermon to a periodical that specializes
in bare boobs.

"I try not to commit a deliberate sin," he told the magazine. "I
recognize that I'm going to do it anyhow, because I'm human and
I'm tempted. And Christ set some almost impossible standards for
us. Christ said, 'I tell you that anyone who looks on a woman with
lust has in his heart already committed adultery.'

"I've looked on a lot of women with lust. I've committed adultery in my heart many times. This is something that God recog-
nizes I will do—and I have done it—and God forgives me for it."

By declaring his technical purity (and securing God's permission), Carter almost seems to be presciently distancing himself from the whole Bill Clinton and Monica Lewinsky mess that would strangle the White House two decades hence. It did nothing for his reputation, however. Clinton the Cheater was wildly popular in spite of, or maybe because of, his sexual transgressions. But after four years in office, Carter the Limp couldn't get elected town dog catcher. Carter's impotence, real or figurative, was a theme that would dominate his presidency from its very first day, January 20, 1977, when Carter, accompanied by wife Rosalynn and daughter Amy, chose to walk, instead of ride, along the inauguration route in Washington, D.C. Carter wanted to be seen as a man of the people. But the public wants a virile, mythical figure, not a waffling peanut farmer who couldn't make up his mind to save the nation.

> *Carter wanted to be seen as a man of the people. But the public wants a virile, mythical figure, not a waffling peanut farmer who couldn't make up his mind to save the nation.*

As president, Jimmy Carter could not catch a break, and probably didn't deserve one. The Carter era was a time of huge inflation and snaking gas lines. People slept in their cars in order to be in front of a pump as soon as stations opened and just as quickly ran out of fuel. It also was the time when the Soviet Union invaded Afghanistan. Carter responded to this threat by keeping United States athletes out of the Moscow Olympics in 1980, as well as by instituting aid to the Islamist Afghanis, a policy, continued under the Reagan administration, whose full disastrous impact would be known two decades later.

CARTER EXTENDED AN open-arms policy to all Cubans who wanted sanctuary in the United States from Fidel Castro's country. It would be an unmitigated embarrassment. Between April and October 1980, some 125,000 Cubans washed up on our shores in the Mariel boatlift. As it turned out, a good number of these so-called refugees were released from Castro's prisons and mental institutions, flooding Scarfaces and freaks onto the streets of Miami.

BUT FOR ALL the failures for which Carter is remembered, the absolute nadir was reached in the final year of his presidency, when sixty-six hostages were seized by militants in the United States embassy in Tehran, Iran. Fifty-two were held captive an astonishing 444 days, an embarrassment that crippled the limping Carter presidency, as a band of Iranian thugs made the all-powerful United States government look like the Keystone Kops. Only one rescue attempt was planned, and even this was aborted at the very last second. Even so, on April 25, 1980, the military rescue helicopter collided with a refueling plane in the Iranian desert. Pandemonium erupted as United States servicemen believed they were under enemy attack. Eight were killed. Though the hostages were held another nine months, no rescue attempt was made. Carter was so unpopular toward the end of his presidency, he was challenged by Teddy Kennedy for the 1980 Democratic nomination, but somehow stubbornly emerged as the party's standard bearer. In the end, he was defeated in the general election by Republican Ronald Reagan. The day Reagan was sworn in to office also was the day the hostages were released from Iran.

What is a failed politician to do? It is a theme that would crop up more than two decades later with Al Gore, when he lost a White House he thought he owned. Some men in Carter's position might slink into bitter obscurity, return to farming, and be forgotten. But for some reason known only to him, Jimmy Carter believed his gifts were too valuable to squander, whether or not the public wanted them. And so, Jimmy Carter set out to save the world. Whether or not the world wanted him.

Carter did high-profile volunteer work with Habitat for Humanity, helping low-income people build and purchase houses. He set up the Carter Center to advance human rights and promote health care. But despite boldly putting his name on his work, he was unsatisfied with the role of global do-gooder. As president, Carter negotiated a peace treaty between Israel and Egypt. He knew that conducting foreign policy was the key to fame, renewed relevancy, and impossible-to-get reservations at his restaurant of choice, even if it meant he must meddle, irritatingly, at the adult table. But Carter appears to have been born lacking the gene for shame. Despite his reputation as a learned man, he also has developed a keen ability to ignore all facts except those that might generate buzz.

Carter has angered President Bill Clinton and both Presidents Bush by his meddling, freelance diplomacy. He persuaded Clinton to let him visit North Korea in 1994 where he negotiated an agreement under which that country agreed to stop processing nuclear fuel. For his efforts, Carter won the 2002 Nobel Peace Prize—rapidly shaping up as the consolation prize for failed, lefty politicians—for his work in bringing peace to places from Haiti to North Korea. Too bad you can't rescind a Nobel. Within a few years, North Korea was back to making nukes.

Carter ignited outrage when he was seen schmoozing with Cuban leader Fidel Castro during the 2000 funeral of former Canadian prime minister Pierre Trudeau. Not one to be cowed, he visited the island nation in 2002, becoming the first president in or out of office to do so since the Communist revolution of 1959. While in Cuba, Carter met with Castro and addressed the people, in Spanish, on national television.

Castro is not the only avowed enemy of this country with whom Carter has played footsie. He installed himself as an observer of Venezuela's recall election in 2004 after members of the European Union declined the mission, complaining that there were too many restrictions placed upon them by the administration of Hugo Chavez. Though some of the American press and pollsters reported massive fraud at the polls, Carter insisted that Chavez, an avid Socialist with a miserable record of human rights abuses, was the proper winner. When Chavez stood on the floor of the United Nations and called President Bush "diablo [devil]," one can only assume Carter approved.

Carter was on a roll. In March 2004, he went after President Bush and British Prime Minister Tony Blair for waging war to oust Iraqi butcher Saddam Hussein "based upon lies and misinterpretations." Then he upped the volume. Asked in 2007 how he would judge Blair's support of Bush, he responded, "Abominable. Loyal. Blind. Apparently subservient."

And then, he outdid himself. In an interview published May 19, 2007, in the *Arkansas Democrat-Gazette*, he said, "I think as far as the adverse impact on the nation around the world, this administration has been the worst in history. The overt reversal of America's basic values as expressed by previous administrations, including those of George H.W. Bush and Ronald Reagan and Richard Nixon and others, has been the most disturbing to me."

Tulane University historian and Carter biographer Douglas Brinkley called Carter's "worst in history" remark unprecedented. Shocking.

"When you call somebody the worst president, that's volatile. Those are fighting words," he said.

The next day, White House spokesman Tony Fratto dismissed Carter's flailing as so much grousing from a loser. "I think it's sad that President Carter's reckless personal criticism is out there. I think it's unfortunate. And I think he is proving to be increasingly irrelevant with these kinds of comments." Ouch.

Maybe Carter knew he'd blown it. Days later, Carter blamed others for "misinterpreting" what he clearly said. He told the *Today* show that the words "were maybe careless or misinterpreted." He said he "certainly was not talking personally about any president." This would not be the last time that Carter, when asked to defend bloviations spewing from his mouth or emanating recklessly from his pen, would try to take them back. Sort of.

Nothing Carter has ever done or said, no matter how hurtful or ridiculous, could compare with his book, *Palestine: Peace Not Apartheid.*

Carter pathetically tried to attract attention, even enmity, with his comparison of Israel and South Africa's former apartheid system, in which the separation of the races was written into law. But this comparison just doesn't fly in Israel. In the Jewish state, many Palestinians are full citizens. But Carter didn't care.

Even more frighteningly, he suggested that Americans tend to get their information from the Jewish-dominated media, which he claimed silences opposition voices. That's a dangerous absurdity that feeds into any number of conspiracy theories that have been used historically as an excuse to put down Jews. In truth, these days many leftist pundits and politicians are downright hostile to Israel. But Carter omitted and twisted facts that did not meet his thesis.

A furor erupted over the book, as fifteen people resigned in disgust from the advisory board of the Atlanta-based Carter Center. Kenneth Stein, an adviser to Carter for twenty-three years, walked away after calling the book "replete with factual errors, copied materials not cited"—an alarming claim—"superficialities, glaring omissions and simply invented segments." In another interview, Stein said that Carter had "taken [material] directly" from a previously published work. He got no reply from Carter.

Even then-House Minority Leader Nancy Pelosi issued a statement: "With all due respect to former President Carter, he does not speak for the Democratic Party on Israel. Democrats have been steadfast in their support of Israel from its birth, in part because we recognize that to do so is in the national security interests of the United States. We stand with Israel now and we stand with Israel forever. The Jewish people know what it means to be oppressed, discriminated against, and even condemned to death because of their religion. They have been leaders in the fight for human rights in the United States and throughout the world. It is wrong to suggest that the Jewish people would support a government in Israel or anywhere else that institutionalizes technically based on oppression, and Democrats reject that allegation vigorously." Tell 'em, Nancy.

Well, did Carter mean "apartheid" or not? At the end of 2006, Carter wrote an open letter to the Jewish community, in which he stated that "apartheid in Palestine is not based on racism but the desire of a minority of Israelis for Palestinian land and the resulting suppression of protests that involve violence." He also defended himself from charges (deserved) that he had suggested that Jews control the news media. He insisted, "I have never claimed that American Jews control the news media, but reiterated that the overwhelming bias for Israel comes from among Christians like me who have been taught since childhood to honor and protect God's chosen people from among whom came our own savior, Jesus Christ." OK, then, "Apartheid" is neither accurate nor defensible. So why use the word?

Ethan Bronner, the *New York Times'* deputy foreign editor, used the Gray Lady's pages to pen a devastating review of Carter's book in January 2007.

Bronner blasted the book as being "premised on the notion that Americans too often get only one side of the story, one uncritically sympathetic to Israel, so someone with authority and knowledge needs to offer a fuller picture. Fine idea. The problem is that in this book Jimmy Carter does not do so. Instead, he simply offers a narrative that is largely unsympathetic to Israel. Israeli bad faith fills the pages. Hollow statements by Israel's enemies are presented without comment. Broader regional developments go largely unexamined. In other words, whether or not Carter is right that most Americans have a distorted view of the conflict, his contribution is to offer a distortion of his own."

Bronner does not dispute that many Palestinians live in substandard conditions. But the good in the book, he wrote, is erased by the author's refusal to see what is happening in the Middle East. "For the most radical leaders of the Muslim world—and their numbers are not dwindling—settling the Israel question does not mean an equitable division of land between Israel and Palestine. It means eliminating Israel."

Ultimately, he disputes the notion that Carter is anti-Semitic, concluding that the former president sees everything through the prism of a devout Christian, which makes him tone deaf to the shouts and murmurs of the region. It's an optimistic assessment. And one I don't share.

From whence does Carter's loyalty to Arab causes arise? When did his distrust, bordering on rabid hatred, of Israel commence? Could it be a simple matter of dollars and cents?

Harvard law professor Alan Dershowitz, who was once counted as a Carter adviser, reported in *Front Page* magazine that Carter's foundation has drunk up untold millions in oil money from the Middle East, especially from Saudi Arabia. Carter even received a monetary reward in the name of Sheikh Zayed bin Sultan al-Nahayan. Dershowitz himself persuaded Harvard to return $2 million of this man's dirty money when he learned that the Zayed Centre for Coordination called the Holocaust a "fable," claimed Israel assassinated President John F. Kennedy and the United States was responsible for the 9/11 attacks. His organization also hosted speakers who called Jews "enemies of all nations." And still, Carter took money from this character, saying, "This award has special significance for me because it is named for my personal friend, Sheik Zayed bin Sultan al-Nahyan."

"I sadly concluded that Jimmy Carter of the twenty-first century has become complicit in evil," Dershowitz wrote. "Carter and his Center have accepted millions of dollars from suspect sources, beginning with the bail-out of the Carter family peanut business in the late 1970s by BCCI, a now-defunct and virulently anti-Israeli bank indirectly controlled by the Saudi Royal family, and among whose principal investors is Carter's friend, Sheikh Zayed."

Carter received $500,000 from the bank's founder, Agha Hasan Abedi, who has doled out more than $10 million for Carter's projects. Carter took the money, overlooking Abedi's statement that his bank is "the best way to fight the evil influence of the Zionists."

And thus, Carter has set himself up as the biggest hypocrite of modern times. He blasts "Jewish money" for warping coverage of the Middle East in favor of Israel, while never fully disclosing the fact that Jimmy Carter is a wholly owned subsidiary of the Arab world.

"By Carter's own standards, therefore, his views on the Middle East must be discounted," wrote Dershowitz. And still, Jimmy Carter presses on.

One might think of Jimmy Carter as the terrorists' pal. But in April 2008, he went one better. Jimmy Carter became the terrorists' tool.

Defying officials of his own government as well as Israel's who warned Carter against providing aid and comfort to the enemy, Carter staged a Middle Eastern tour of favorite terrorist haunts. And so, Carter's role in foreign politics matured. For years, he'd played sidelines agitator. Now he'd emerged as a full-blown collaborator.

Arriving in the West Bank town of Ramallah with wife Rosalynn, he hugged and kissed on both cheeks Nasser Shaer, a former deputy prime minister in the Hamas-led (read: terrorist) government. He praised the late terror-monger and thief Yasser Arafat and solemnly laid a wreath on his grave, while praising him for championing causes that are just (he didn't mention Arafat's wholesale looting of the Palestinian treasury). Naturally, he accused Israel of holding up the latest peace negotiations.

He tried to get to Gaza, but Israel wouldn't help him. In fact, officials shunned him. So at a Cairo hotel, he met with Mahmud al-Zahar, who masterminded the Hamas seizure of the Gaza Strip. Al-Zahar got so juiced from the drop-in, he declared that Carter's presence was a blow to the United States' boycott of Hamas.

In Damascus, he topped himself. Despite warnings from State Department officials in the United States who feared Carter would breathe legitimacy to butchers, he met top exiled leaders of Hamas, Khaled Mashaal and Moussa Abu Marzuk. These men are labeled global terrorists by the United States. These men are at the top of Israel's most-wanted list.

Evidently, reasoning with Carter is fruitless. A source close to Carter told Reuters news service that the notoriety of his mission only encouraged him to go further.

Pressed about playing nice with killers, Carter got cute. He insisted that he was only visiting terror haunts as a private citizen. "I'm not a negotiator. I'm just trying to understand different opinions and provide communication between people," he said.

Then, Jimmuh *really* stepped in it.

Following his terrorist tour with a trip to Wales in May 2008, Carter dropped a nuclear bomb. He became the first American who might be in a position to know to declare that Israel possessed at least 150 nuclear weapons—something Israel has never admitted, and Americans have never discussed. Well, he's Jimmy Carter, enemy of the Jewish state.

He said this by way of arguing that the United States should try to persuade Iran to dump its nuclear ambitions. But observers noted that Carter might push Iran to start producing nukes for real. Carter's outrageously loose lips may have put lives in peril. Finally, the public might begin to see that, for Jimmy Carter, that's the whole point.

I'm afraid Jimmy Carter is something far worse than a simple
Jew hater: he is a situational anti-Semite. One with no deep feelings in his heart about the matter. He is an opportunist.

The $64,000 question is—Did Carter actually condone terrorist
attacks against Israel? Here is the wording on page 213 of *Palestine:
Peace Not Apartheid*, as Carter wrote it:

"It is imperative that the general Arab community and all significant Palestinian groups make it clear that they will end the suicide bombings and other acts of terrorism when international laws
and the ultimate goals of the road map for peace are accepted by Israel."

There you have it. Jimmy Carter was stating, unequivocally,
that Palestinian terror is a deserved consequence of Israel's actions,
and would not stop unless and until Israel caves in to their de-
mands. Absurd. Ridiculous. Stupid. And guaranteed to resonate
with those who despise Israel. With those who would like to wipe
Israel off the map.

He must have realized he'd gone too far. Carter told National
Public Radio: "That was a terribly worded sentence which implied,
obviously in a ridiculous way, that I approved terrorism and terrorist acts against Israeli citizens."

He continued: "The 'when' was obviously a crazy and stupid
word. My publishers have been informed about that and have
changed the sentence in all future editions of the book."

"Crazy and stupid." He said it. I didn't. Sadly, the uproar did
not have the intended effect. It just helped fuel Carter's publicity
machine.

To this day, Jimmy Carter has never fully explained how this
distortion, in addition to so many other falsehoods and libels, made
it into his book in the first place. I have come to a conclusion about
Jimmy Carter, and his constant need to shock, then backtrack,
then stand by so many offensive statements: He'll say anything to
prevent returning to the dust bin of history's trash can, where he
belongs.

14

The Color Green
OPRAH WINFREY

It's amazing grace that brought me here. Amazing grace.
> —Oprah Winfrey with presidential candidate Barack Obama
> in South Carolina, December 9, 2007

To me, it seems to be much ado about nothing
> —Oprah defending author James Frey to Larry King,
> January 11, 2006

*James Frey is here and I have to say it is difficult for me
to talk to you because I feel really duped. But more
importantly, I feel that you betrayed millions of readers.*
> —Slamming author James Frey on *The Oprah Winfrey Show*,
> January 26, 2006

*I understand why people think we're gay. There isn't
a definition in our culture for this kind of bond between
women. So I get why people have to label it—how
can you be this close without it being sexual?*
> —Oprah in *O* magazine on her relationship with best buddy
> Gayle King, August 2006

I have to admit, if Oprah were a man, I would marry her.
—Gayle King in *O*, August 2006

THE MOST POWERFUL WOMAN in America was not born rich or royal. She was never elected or appointed to office, nor did she inherit, marry or steal her incredible wealth, vast influence and international fame. This woman is capable of minting superstars, moving millions in merchandise and anointing political candidates with a wave of her hand and a nod of her head. When she opens her mouth, millions listen. She is Oprah Winfrey. She is our queen.

Perhaps I understate Oprah's power. CNN and *Time* have labeled her arguably the most influential woman in the world. She accomplished this feat not through conventional means, such as running for politics or staging a bloody coup, but through today's reigning pseudo-government: the media-infotainment-industrial complex. Oprah, a former Academy Award–nominated actress and TV reporter turned magazine publisher, hosts the highest-rated talk show in television history. Lest you think daytime TV is mainly for bored housewives and unemployed ex-cons, think again. Politicians and authors seek Oprah's counsel. Starlets compete for her praise. A word of condemnation from Oprah's mouth can cost your business millions. But winning Oprah's seal of approval can more than make your career. It can make life worth living.

That a dirt-poor black girl from the deep South might rise to become America's billionaire sweetheart (her net worth has been estimated at $2.5 billion, far more than any other African-American) is a head-scratcher. She is bright, but not brilliant. Educated. But not too. Her tastes are decidedly middle-brow. But Oprah's struggles—particularly with her ever-fluctuating weight—have only made her more appealing to vast numbers of housewives and career women.

These days, giving the illusion of intimate confession is as good as the real thing, and Oprah has found common ground with all manner of people who believe she truly understands their complaints. These are people not accustomed to thinking too hard for themselves.

I wish I could maintain that Oprah is harmless. But some of the campaigns she has waged over the years, from defending an author who faked his life's story, to championing Madonna's putative purchase of an African baby, to campaigning for a hard leftist such as Barack Obama in his run for president of the United States, have left me gasping.

She was born Oprah Gail Winfrey in rural Mississippi on January 29, 1954, to a poor, unwed teen mother who worked as a housemaid. Or was she? In a 1991 interview, she said she was actually named "Orpah," after the Biblical character, Ruth's sister-in-law, but that her family and friends were incapable of pronouncing the name and it was changed to "Oprah."

The story of her early life is Dickensian, punctuated by inspirational moments of genuine triumph. In fact, her story unspools like a made-for-TV movie. You can't make this stuff up.

For Oprah's first six years, she lived in rural poverty with her strict, devout grandmother, Hattie Mae, who taught young Oprah to read before the age of three and did not spare the switch. Oprah's mother Vernita Lee then took her to live in a Milwaukee slum. Oprah has said she was raped by a cousin at the age of nine, and molested by an uncle and by a male friend of her mother's. In other interviews, she's said she was molested at four, which would have placed her at her grandmother's house.

While under her mother's tutelage, she repeatedly ran away and got into trouble. Vernita Lee sent her to live with her father, Vernon Winfrey, a coal miner and barber who was elected to the city council in Nashville, Tennessee. At age fourteen, Oprah gave birth to a son who died in infancy. She was devastated. Oprah never again gave birth to a child.

Vernon Winfrey was a strict man who made education a priority in his daughter's life. While still in high school, Oprah took a job in radio, and enrolled in Tennessee State University at age seventeen.

During her freshman year, she entered the beauty pageant circuit and was named Miss Black Nashville as well as Miss Tennessee. At nineteen, she became a local TV news co-anchor on WLAC-TV. In 1976, Oprah moved to Baltimore, where she co-anchored the six o'clock news on WJZ-TV. She then was offered the job as co-host of the local talk show, *People Are Talking*, and hosted *Dialing for Dollars*.

Oprah moved to Chicago in 1983 to host a morning talk show on WLS-TV, which quickly rose from the ratings cellar to beat the better established *Donahue* program. Oprah's show went national, and was renamed *The Oprah Winfrey Show*. Twenty years later, Oprah revealed that movie critic Roger Ebert, with whom she was involved, persuaded her to sign a syndication deal with King World, a move that was unusual for the time, but would make Oprah rich beyond her wildest imagination. Chicago would become the show's permanent base, though Oprah would buy many houses. Eventually, her main place of residence became, not surprisingly, California.

It went so fast, and for a reason. Oprah gets roundly criticized for single-handedly lowering the IQ of popular television, dumbing down America even as she pretended to raise it up. It was Oprah who introduced the culture of confession, over-publicizing fad therapies and even unquestioningly giving air time to psychic phenomena and the occult. But the true hallmark of the Age of Oprah is her willingness to grant not just sympathy, but normalcy and understanding, to people who in earlier days would be shunned as freaks, desensitizing Americans to those who live outside societal norms. Oprah was praised for giving airtime to gay, bisexual and transgender individuals (did I leave anyone out?), but slammed by sociologist Vicki Abt, who co-wrote *Coming After Oprah: Cultural Fallout in the Age of the TV Talk Show*, who warned about blurring the lines between normal and deviant behavior.

For better or ill, she rapidly became a cultural force more influential than educational institutions, the family or even the church.

Time magazine said, "Few people would have bet on Oprah Winfrey's swift rise to host one of the most popular talk shows on TV. In a field dominated by white males, she is a black female of ample bulk. As interviewers go, she is no match for, say, Phil Donahue . . . What she lacks in journalistic toughness, she makes up for in plainspoken curiosity, robust humor, and above all, empathy. Guests with sad stories to tell are apt to rouse a tear in Oprah's eye . . . They, in turn, often find themselves revealing things they would not imagine telling anyone, much less a national TV audience. It is the talk show as a group therapy session."

In 1985, she co-starred in Steven Spielberg's film of Alice Walker's novel, *The Color Purple*, and was nominated for a Best Supporting Actress Academy Award for playing Sofia. (She lost to Anjelica Huston.)

Observing that Oprah had become increasingly vocal in her opposition to the war in Iraq, Ben Shapiro of Townhall.com wrote, "Oprah Winfrey is the most powerful woman in America. She decides what makes the *New York Times* best-seller lists. Her touchy-feely style sucks in audiences at the rate of 14 million viewers per day. But Oprah is far more than a cultural force—she's a dangerous political force as well, a woman with unpredictable and mercurial attitudes toward the major issues of the day."

If you would doubt Oprah's power, you're probably not a beef producer. During a 1996 program about mad cow disease with Howard Lyman, Oprah spontaneously exclaimed, "It has just stopped me cold from eating another burger!" Texas cattlemen were not amused, charging that the single comment cost their industry some $12 million. They sued Oprah for "false defamation of perishable food" and "business disparagement" in an Amarillo, Texas, court. The two-month case required Oprah to temporarily relocate her program to Texas. A jury found that Oprah and Lyman were not liable.

With her weight rising and falling—Oprah has blamed this alternately on her insecurity and on a thyroid condition—she once enjoyed a frisky love life, but has settled down for twenty-plus years with Stedman Graham, whom she has never married. They raise dogs. Though many have wondered why the pair never stepped down the aisle, it is Oprah's relationship with her best friend, Gayle King, a former TV host and *O* magazine editor, with whom she has spoken on the phone four times a day for more than thirty years, that has raised the most eyebrows. Rumors that the two women are lesbians have persisted since 1997, when Oprah played the therapist on the episode of *Ellen* in which Ellen DeGeneres came out of the closet. Oprah attempted to put the gay talk to rest in an *O* magazine piece that, frankly, only stoked the fire. "People think I'd be so ashamed of being gay that I wouldn't admit it? Oh, please," she said.

Honestly, just thinking about the man, woman or farm animal with whom Oprah spends her nights leaves me shrugging. I don't care, and I don't believe the majority of Americans do, either. What bothers me a whole heck of a lot more is how Oprah conducts herself with her clothes on. And as she's risen to a level of credibility that's beaten only by the pope—and I'm sure some would disagree with that—she's made some astounding blunders.

> *Honestly, just thinking about the man, woman or farm animal with whom Oprah spends her nights leaves me shrugging.*

The spokesmouth for Oprah's production company, Harpo (Oprah spelled backwards) called this incident her "crash moment." She meant that Oprah suffered an episode of fierce and unjust racism. But I have another description for the event that badly rattled Oprah's cage, spurring her to stage a modern-day struggle to protect her civil rights, and those of all insanely rich celebutards. I call it Oprah's "Do you know who I am?!" moment.

On the evening of June 14, 2005, Oprah and her entourage arrived fifteen minutes past closing time, at the lavishly expensive Hermes boutique in Paris, France, whose signature Birkin handbags start at around $6,000 and rise dizzyingly upward. Staff was in the store, preparing for a public-relations event that night. Oprah wanted inside (to buy a watch for Tina Turner). A clerk told her "Non."

"Do you know who I am?!" Oprah asked.

Denied! A near international incident occurred, as Oprah suggested that if a white celebrity had stopped by after closing, they'd kiss her behind. "I know the difference between a store that is closed and a store that is closed to me," said Oprah. Promises were made to TV viewers that Oprah would discuss on her program the awful racism she endured at a boutique whose name many women can't even pronounce, let alone afford to buy a $320 silk pocket square. Even during regular store hours.

Soon, the Hermes CEO called Oprah's people to explain, and invited the put-out star to come back and shop. I would venture that Oprah could stop in at midnight today and be kissed up to. She created such a stink, Hermes was bullied into issuing this public apology: "Hermes regrets not having been able to accommodate Ms. Winfrey and her team and to provide her with the service and care that Hermes strives to provide to each and every one of its customers worldwide. Hermes apologizes for any offense taken due to such circumstances."

The following September, Hermes USA CEO Robert Chavez appeared on Oprah's show, bowing and scraping and apologizing once again about "rude" treatment by an employee. We should all endure such crash moments.

The introduction of Oprah's Book Club—which has done more than anything since the publication of the Bible to sell paper and ink—leaves me with mixed feelings. On the one hand, I appreciate that someone, particularly a major cultural force, encourages people to shut off the tube, pick up book, and read. On the other, I wonder about the whims and politics of being selected for plugging on Oprah's show. The appearance of one's book on the program routinely means a million additional sales and instant inclusion on best-seller lists. This process has even given rise to a scientific phe-nomenon—The Oprah Effect.

James Frey had no idea what he was getting into when his book, *A Million Little Pieces* was pushed by Oprah, causing it to rocket to the top of Amazon.com. The story of the author's drug and alco-hol addiction and criminality was sold as a memoir. That is, it was supposed to be the truth. In addition to other nail-biting passages, Frey describes being in recovery and undergoing two root canals with no anesthesia, which he withstood by squeezing a tennis ball until his nails cracked.

Of course, later he said he might have had one root canal. With novocaine. Whatever. Oprah was seen as plugging fiction as fact, encouraging Americans to lie, cheat and exaggerate for a buck. It got worse when she called into *Larry King Live* in early 2006 to de-fend Frey, saying the scandal was "much ado about nothing," and suggesting that it was irrelevant if the book was true, as long as Frey's memoir inspired people.

But the symphony of outrage grew only more deafening, and Frey was proclaimed a cynical phony. It was time for Oprah to turn. She lured Frey to her program, where she told him to his face that she felt duped. And she explained to her millions of viewers that Oprah Winfrey would never suggest that the truth doesn't matter. Not mentioned was the fact that, had the book never been "discovered" by Oprah, few people would know or care.

In the end, *A Million Little Pieces* sold tons of copies, no doubt benefiting from the attention. An embarrassing episode. And the entire *megillah* proves one major truth about the publishing indus-try, addiction and Oprah Winfrey: Authors—do anything in your power, and I mean anything, to get mentioned on Oprah's Book Club.

In what may be a case of silly excess—or no good deed goes un-punished—Oprah's $40 million Leadership Academy for Girls near Johannesburg, South Africa, opened to great ridicule. The academy offered 152 impoverished students the opportunity to sleep on high thread-count sheets, to have the use of a beauty salon, indoor and outdoor theater, and attend yoga classes. Oprah was criticized at the school's opening for not offering more modest facilities to educate a larger number of children. But she defended the star treatment as a way to effect long-term change in the troubled nation. In fall 2007, a matron was charged with sexually and physically abusing students, which led Oprah to fly to South Africa to help clean up the mess.

All of this makes me wonder—Is Oprah Winfrey a force for good in the world? Or ill? I chose the latter when I saw her cluck and cheer as she interviewed Madonna on her acquisition of an African baby. To whom else would Mrs. Ritchie speak?

A fuller discussion of the chick chat is found in the Madonna chapter of this book. I'll say here that Oprah was in her mightiest "Bless you!" form when talking, via satellite, to the woman who earned the wrath of human rights groups for snatching a baby from his father and his village so she might accumulate a matched set of kids. Madonna didn't need a lawyer, a priest or a spiritual adviser to get her out of trouble. She needed Oprah—a woman who wouldn't know a tough question if it bit her on sensitive parts of the body. And Oprah approved. Discussion over.

Another human of whom Oprah approves is Barack Obama. As he became the first serious African-American candidate in history to seek the presidency Oprah didn't just support him. She embraced him, idolized him and bestowed upon him the awesome power of Oprah. Who needs endorsements?

In December 2007, Oprah campaigned for Obama in Iowa, New Hampshire, and at a rally in South Carolina, drawing an eye-popping crowd of 30,000, where people carried signs proclaiming, "Oprah for Vice President." Obama was the headline. Oprah was the star.

According to the Politico.com website, Oprah touched not only on religious themes, but at times the South Carolina rally sounded downright messianic. It's not enough, said Oprah, for politicians to tell the truth, "We need politicians who know how to be the truth."

I wonder if, in this age of Oprahtainment, we need to elect leaders at all. All we need is to allow Oprah Winfrey to step up and tell us what to think, to feel, to buy and to say.

She already does.

I wonder if, in this age of Oprahtainment, we need to elect leaders at all. All we need is to allow Oprah Winfrey to step up and tell us what to think, to feel, to buy and to say.

15

All the News That's Sh★t to Print
THE NEW YORK TIMES

I found that the past year's articles generally reported both sides, and that most flaws flowed from journalistic lapses rather than ideological bias.
—Public Editor Byron Calame on his paper's continued championing of the Duke University rape hoax, April 22, 2007

THE NEW YORK TIMES IS a lot more than fish wrap. It is a vaunted institution whose editorials on a daily basis are capable of influencing government and corporate policy, both in the United States and abroad, whose trend stories can move millions of dollars in merchandise, whose news columns are apt to change the current of public discourse, and whose whims and fancies scattered throughout the paper may create and end careers. Or so it claims.

As the self-described newspaper of record, (established 1851) *The Times* proclaims that it publishes "All the news that's fit to print." That is an awesome promise to its readers, and one not to be taken lightly. And so it is to make one scream how often this newspaper has abused and distorted its sacred pages to advance grudges, push political and social agendas, move government policy to the far left, and blithely obscure any version of truth except that practiced

124

in the People's Republic of West 41st Street in its steady march to win the Pulitzer prize, of which *The Times* has taken home a record number.

Examples are legion. The paper has waged tireless campaigns over the years that defy logic and countermand journalistic credibility. *The Times* fought to keep alive the charges against three innocent, white Duke University lacrosse players unfairly accused of raping a black woman, and hinted incredibly about an extramarital affair by Republican presidential candidate John McCain, who was guilty of nothing more than being a Republican.

It was stubborn in its support for the admittance of women to the Augusta National Golf Club, a non-story about which there was virtually no public outcry. During the Nazi regime *The Times* refused to acknowledge mass slaughter, ignoring all evidence of systematic murder until it was far too late to save Jewish lives. These random examples paint a long-term pattern that leads one to believe that the warping of information is no accident. Rather, it is a virulent disease.

> *During the Nazi regime The Times refused to acknowledge mass slaughter, ignoring all evidence of systematic murder until it was far too late to save Jewish lives.*

Due to the paper's many gaffes and missteps, coupled with its transparent left-leaning ideology disguised as objectivity, many have come to question the *Times'* stranglehold on journalistic authority. Still, it is alarming how frequently the paper continues to be cited in other media, or worse, its spins and assertions are parroted, unattributed, in places as disparate as television, newspapers and the Internet. This worldview may benefit the social élan of the paper's editors and reporters, but it does precious little for the truth.

Two examples from the past illustrate this point. The first is the story of a renegade reporter who traded the truth for a Pulitzer and a place of honor at a tyrant's table. The second is of a publisher so ashamed of his faith, he would let his own brethren die so as not to rock the boat.

Few examples illustrate the *Times'* stubborn argument with stark reality as clearly as the case of Walter Duranty, the Soviet Union correspondent in the 1930s. Duranty was both an apologist for Josef Stalin and a bit of a tyrant, appointing himself America's cheerleader for a regime whose farm collectivization policies were responsible for the famine that ripped through Ukraine, piling uncounted millions of bodies into town squares. Duranty, a one-legged reporter—he'd lost a limb in a car crash—claimed, among other things, that brutal Siberian labor camps gave people a chance to rejoin Soviet society and, for those who couldn't fit in, "the final fate of such enemies is death."

Reports of a Ukranian famine began appearing in other newspapers in 1932, but Duranty was in public denial. Without television or Internet pictures to give lie to his reporting, he was considered by many the final authority. For his bloodthirsty work, he was awarded the Pulitzer Prize in 1932.

But in a private conversation with a British diplomat in 1933, Duranty admitted, "it is quite possible that as many as 10 million people may have died directly or indirectly from lack of food in the Soviet Union during the past year." Still, Duranty continued to lie about the non-existence of mass starvation as he curried favor with the Soviets. Much later, several organizations demanded that the Pulitzer board revoke Duranty's prize, but in 2003, the organization officially declined. This prize will always have an asterisk attached. How many more?

Just a few years later, the paper's publisher, Arthur Hays Sulzberger, was considered primarily responsible for the paper's downplaying of reports from Europe that Adolf Hitler's Third Reich was targeting Jews for expulsion—and genocide. Sulzberger, a Jew, feared taking on any Jewish cause. Once again, it will never be clear how many lives may have been saved through a well-placed story, a

Page 1 photo, or how American foreign policy may have been influenced for the good, had our Newspaper of Record done its job.

Fast forward to the present. The *Times*' long-term hostility toward the military was undeniable in an extreme act of omission in October 2007. Alone among local dailies, the paper printed not a word of President George W. Bush's plan to bestow the Medal of Honor to a New Yorker who gave his life to save another in Afghanistan. Fully ten days after the medal was announced, garnering coverage from reporters from the *Denver Post* and *Los Angeles Times*, as well as by scribes at all the other New York papers, *The Times* published a short (for *The Times*) article about Bush actually awarding the medal. A longer piece appeared a month later, hidden in the weekly section that appears only on Long Island.

Any lingering doubts about the *Times*' hostility toward soldiers were eliminated on January 13, 2008, when the paper published a front-page story, which jumped to three inside pages, based around an alarming trend: Fighting men returning from Iraq and Afghanistan had been charged with 121 murders in the United States! However, bloggers and journalists such as columnist Ralph Peters crunched the numbers, and determined the soldiers' murder rate was actually fives times lower than that of the general young male population, a fact *The Times* carelessly—or intentionally?—ignored. Even when you factor in veterans charged but not convicted of deadly crimes, the proportion of potential killers was far lower than that of the non-vet population. Perhaps the paper was irked by progress in Iraq. War casualties had fallen greatly, and with America's help, the country appeared to be returning to a semblance of normalcy. What was left to complain about?

The state of Israel is another frequent *Times* target. In 2007, it published an exhaustive front-page article bemoaning the killing by Israeli soldiers of dozens of Palestinian "children." Never mind that some of these kids were 19 and armed. The piece never mentioned atrocities carried out against Israel by Palestinians.

In 1994, I had the privilege of traveling to South Africa to cover the historical election of Nelson Mandela as the country's first black president. It became immediately clear that the story was more complicated than it initially appeared. Far more than *The Times* insisted.

The election was presented in this country as the force of light—the African National Congress party, led by Mandela—against the force of evil—the Inkatha Freedom party, populated by the vast, poverty-stricken Zulu nation. It was clear Mandela, a good man whose fans in the United States included Jane Fonda and Oprah Winfrey, would win. However, the Zulus were demonized, presented to *Times* readers as collaborators with the forces of Apartheid. It was partly true. Some Zulus in fact teamed up with the white man, mainly as a method to foil the ANC, whose leaders, they felt, were leaving them to starve. It was politics. It was complicated. It was a story *The Times* either failed to understand fully, or found preferable to ignore. And it was a theme I would see regurgitated from *The Times* in papers all over the country, unable to send their own correspondents to cover this news event. It was *Times* Truth.

Bill Keller, the *Times'* Pulitzer winner (for work in the Soviet Union), and later the paper's executive editor, was the Johannesburg correspondent. From his desk in Jo-burg, it was easy to make monsters out of the millions of members of the once-proud Zulu nation, many of them barefoot. Then a funny thing happened. Keller visited the Zulu nation. Here, a century before, warriors defeated the better-equipped British army. Now, people begged for scraps.

His coverage of the election suddenly did a 180-degree turn. He never again denigrated this tribe.

At home, journalistic gospel is far trickier to adjust, particularly if your paper's liberal reputation is on the line. *The Times* waged a long and strenuous battle against the reforming of welfare—the culture of entitlement—that, in 1994, saw 5.1 million American families dependent on public assistance. Because of welfare, generations of children were sentenced to grow up without ever seeing an adult family member go to work.

The Times predicted dire consequences if President Bill Clinton signed the Welfare Reform Act of 1996, putting a five-year limit on benefits. Poverty! Starvation! Rotten jobs! In every scary article, I noticed, the same six anti-reform activists were interviewed. Not one of its reporters actually went to Harlem, East New York or the Bronx—or simply stepped outside the door in Times Square—to talk to the people actually on welfare. So I tried something radical. I did just that.

In Harlem, I asked a mother if reforming welfare would be a hardship. Hell yes! she answered—and the best thing that ever happened to her.

I was in shock. On the street, I talked to various people, men and women, and I could not find a welfare recipient who voiced opposition to reform. They had strong opinions. They knew which of their neighbors was a welfare cheat, they knew how to work the system to their best advantage. They knew how to game it. But everyone I spoke to was excited at the prospect of getting back to work, even in a low-paying job. It sure beat life on the dole.

From its high of more than 5.1 million families on welfare, today fewer than 2 million receive benefits. What's more, rates of poverty among African-American children have dropped dramatically. Welfare reform is a smashing success. Do you think *The Times* ever admitted it was wrong?

The twenty-month reign of *Times'* executive editor and Pulitzer winner (for an essay on his black maid) Howell Raines, which began in September 2001, demonstrates the ease with which the paper can and will run amok.

Raines' catchphrase was "flood the zone"—a term that refers to enlisting all available resources—news reporters, columnists, sports writers, even editorial writers—to cover a story he liked. Even a nonstory.

Raines did just that with his paper's exhaustive coverage of the male-only Augusta National Golf Club in 2002 and 2003, and the skirmish fought against it by one woman, Martha Burk of the National Council of Women's Organizations. This was a story that made Raines' pulse race, and he tried desperately to equate the club's membership policies with the whites-only water fountains of his Southern youth. The subject garnered daily stories, Page 1 think pieces, even articles on the sports pages, editorials and op-ed columns, as *The Times* put pressure on sponsors to pull their support of the Masters tournament in Augusta. But when two columns were written that defended the golf course, they were killed. The paper's lock-step coverage of a story that just wasn't that important was an embarrassment. And it was a precursor to Raines' biggest debacle: Jayson Blair.

Critics, including some inside *The Times*, see Jayson Blair, who is African-American, as a poster boy for the failure of affirmative action. Others say he is a failure of the *Times'* star system, which gives breaks to reporters favored by editors. I say he is simply a failure.

The fact that Jayson Blair single-handedly hoodwinked the grand institution for as long as he did, committing sloppy, plagiarized work—or published stuff he simply made up in his feverish head—speaks volumes about what's wrong with The Times.

But the fact that Jayson Blair single-handedly hoodwinked the grand institution for as long as he did, committing sloppy, plagiarized work—or published stuff he simply made up in his feverish head—speaks volumes about what's wrong with *The Times*. And despite safeguards taken in his wake, signs persist that Blair could happen again.

He started as an intern. Although his work was error-ridden from the start, he was hired as a Metro section reporter. His poor work habits and general flouting of authority led his editor, Jonathan Landman, to send a now-infamous memo warning management "to stop Jayson from writing for *The New York Times*. Right now." He was promoted to the national desk in 2002 instead, and assigned to a high-profile story: the Beltway sniper attacks—a series of terrifying shootings in the Washington, D.C., area that held the region hostage. There, Blair's exclusive reporting threatened the case before it even got close to trial.

Three weeks after the attacks began, two suspects were arrested: John Allen Muhammad, a former Army demolitions expert and expert rifleman, age forty-one, and Lee Boyd Malvo, age seventeen. Blair wrote a series of scoops in which he asserted that Malvo, not Muhammad, was considered by authorities the shooter and the older man the lookout. In one memorable article, Blair actually wrote—and *The New York Times* printed—that a key piece of evidence was "DNA linked to Mr. Malvo that was found on a grape stem dropped at one of the sites where a bullet was fired." That this did not strike some editor as ridiculous is testament to an old saying in journalism: Don't let facts get in the way of a good story.

Blair seemed to be itching to get caught, and he did. In Timesian fashion, the paper commemorated his implosion with a massive report by a committee of twenty-five *Times* staffers and three outside journalists. Published on May 11, 2003, the committee's account uncovered, among other things, that Blair claimed he traveled to Palestine, West Virginia, to interview Gregory Lynch, the father of Private First Class Jessica Lynch, rescued from captivity by U.S. forces. Lynch "choked up as he stood on his porch here overlooking the tobacco fields and cattle pastures, and declared that he remained optimistic," Blair wrote. Trouble was, no tobacco fields or cows can be seen from Lynch's porch. Blair, who wrote this dispatch from the Starbucks near his home in Brooklyn, sought the most clichéd description possible of what he thought West Virginia must look like.

Blair did not self-destruct without taking others down with him: Raines and managing editor Gerald Boyd resigned under pressure. As a result of Blair, the paper created the position of public editor to answer readers' concerns, a fairly useless invention.

I wish I could say Blair's dismissal cleaned up the paper. Far from it. If anything, its campaigns became far more strident and personal.

The case of the Duke rape fiasco remains the prime illustration for how a stubborn paper will never back down, never apologize. Not even after it sought to ruin the lives of three men who did nothing amiss, except associate with the wrong stripper.

Her name was Crystal Gail Mangum. On March 13, 2006, Mangum, age twenty-seven, a college student, and another woman, were hired to dance for members of the Duke University lacrosse team at a house in Durham. It was soon clear that Mangum, who was intoxicated and argued with her customers, was not going to do what she was paid for. Stumbling, she repaired to the bathroom. A short while later, she cried rape.

The story was irresistible, and the Durham district attorney, Mike Nifong, who was up for re-election, blasted the awful details far and wide. Here was the tale of two poor women—one African-American, the other part Asian—students from the wrong side of the tracks, reduced to stripping for privileged white men. When the party got out of hand, the story goes, Mangum was raped.

But Mangum's tale of sexual debauchery and racism started falling apart almost immediately. She told many conflicting stories. Even factoring in confusion, two things could not be ignored: She picked the Duke players out of a photo lineup that included only white lacrosse players. This lineup did not, as United States Department of Justice guidelines insist, include "filler" photos of men who are not considered suspects. In other words, Mangum was given a "multiple-choice test in which there were no wrong answers," defense attorneys charged.

In addition, surveillance footage from a nearby bank machine puts one of the suspects far from the house at the time of the alleged attack. No matter. The time of the attack was simply changed by Nifong.

On April 18, 2006, two lacrosse team members, Collin Finnerty, age twenty, and Reade Seligmann, age twenty, were nonetheless arrested on rape, kidnapping and sexual offense charges. They were joined in May by Duke graduate David Evans, age twenty-three.

The juicy story was just too good to be true. By late spring, nearly every major newspaper in the country had reported it as a case in trouble. Nifong, though, could not let go. And he found an ally in *The New York Times*.

The Times weighed in on August 25, 2006, with a lengthy story based on what it called new evidence. It was a humdinger. And here is the paragraph—the so-called "nut graf"—contained in the 5,700-word Page 1 article. It said everything:

"By disclosing pieces of evidence favorable to the defendants, the defense has created an image of a case heading for the rocks. But an examination of the entire 1,850 pages of evidence gathered by the prosecution in the four months after the accusation yields a more ambiguous picture. It shows that while there are big weaknesses in Mr. Nifong's case, there is also a body of evidence to support his decision to take the matter to a jury."

This groundbreaking report was based largely on brand new, handwritten notes that sprang from the memory of Durham police investigator Robert Gottlieb. They contradicted every other investigator's account. These notes, made at Nifong's request, conveniently fit every theory advanced by the desperate DA. Should they be treated with suspicion?

It is stunning to see how other media fall in line when *The Times* puts its full weight behind Page 1. I watched as Jeffrey Toobin, CNN's legal analyst, regurgitated the *Times'* conclusions—"Nifong," he said, "certainly had more evidence, which would be revealed at trial."

Of course, there never was a trial. And the only evidence Nifong ultimately revealed was the depths of his own depravity.

He withheld from defense attorneys and the press the fact that semen from several other men—none of them a Duke lacrosse player—was found in Mangum's body on the night of the alleged attack. That he kept this information secret was a blow from which the DA would not recover.

On December 22, 2006, Nifong dropped rape charges against the young men. And on April 11, 2007—more than a year after the ordeal began—North Carolina Attorney General Roy Cooper dropped remaining kidnapping and sexual offense charges, declaring the accused men "innocent." Nifong was disbarred.

Times public editor Byron Calame had an opportunity to set the record straight. Perhaps apologize. He did nothing of the kind. He smugly defended his paper's egregious coverage, writing in his column that it was tarred by journalistic lapses—never ideological ones.

Or could it be that white students from well-to-do-families will forever be suspect in the eyes of the *Times*?

In February 2008, *The Times* published a 3,000-word front-page piece that suggested with all the breathlessness of a romance novel that Republican presidential candidate John McCain just might have had an "inappropriate relationship" with a younger, blonde "female lobbyist," Vicki Iseman.

Here's the "nut graf": "A female lobbyist had been turning up with him at fund-raisers, visiting his offices and accompanying him on a client's corporate jet. Convinced the relationship had become romantic, some of his top advisers intervened to protect the candidate from himself—instructing staff members to block the woman's access, privately warning her away, and repeatedly confronting him—several people involved in the campaign said on condition of anonymity."

The sexist language said it all. Reverse the sexes, and would *The Times* have said a "male lobbyist" behaved this way?

So had John McCain turned into Hugh Hefner—or Bill Clinton? Well, *The Times* didn't say. It didn't know. That did not stop the Paper of Record from printing a hatchet job about a member of a class it holds in the esteem of all rich, white men: Republicans.

Oddly, the hit piece ended up helping McCain. *The Times* received thousands of complaints, including many from Democrats and Independents. Following the piece's publication, McCain raised more campaign contributions than ever before.

It was not the result *The New York Times* intended.

The Times did its best to redeem itself the following March. On its Web site, it broke a damning and uncharacteriscally tabloidy story about New York's Democratic governor who was caught with his pants down being serviced by a ring of prostitutes whose fees start at $1,000 an hour. His latest flame was just four years older than his daughter. The governor, Eliot Spitzer, resigned in disgrace two days later.

Wouldn't you know it? Some elements within the *Times* seemed embarrassed by the sexy story. As the paper prepared to run its biggest scoop of the year, executive editor Bill Keller took off for Paris.

16

The Mouth That Roared
ROSIE O'DONNELL

Don't fear the terrorists. They're mothers and fathers.
—Rosie O'Donnell on *The View*, November 2006

I HAVE A GUILTY little secret. I genuinely like Rosie O'Donnell. Or I did.

I bonded with the foul-mouthed, overweight, lesbian mama and 9/11 denier in 2003, as she stood trial in a civil case held in the dank and dusty bowels of Manhattan Supreme Court, an old behemoth of a structure that looks grand from the outside, but inside is so dirty and depressing, you wouldn't want to touch the banisters without preventive medication. It was here that Rosie was sued by German-owned publisher Gruner + Jahr USA for $100 million, after Rosie walked away from the editor's job at a magazine that was once *McCall's*, but was renamed *Rosie* in her honor.

Out of a day job at the time, Rosie countersued G+J for $125 million, and I supposed she could use all the media friends she could get. Contrary to popular belief, I do have a heart. And Rosie—unscripted, unguarded and, it seemed, refreshingly real, came to court all dolled up in bright red, in contrast to the suits trotted out by G+J, in various shades from slate to asphalt. She won my loyalty. We became buds. Looking back, I guess Rosie played me. Well, I wasn't exactly hard to get.

Roseann Theresa O'Donnell was born March 21, 1962, in Bayside, in the borough of Queens, New York—the very place in which I also was raised, though I didn't know this when I met her. She was the third of five children born to Edward and Roseann O'Donnell, who died of breast cancer four days before Rosie's eleventh birthday. Rosie was raised in Commack, on Long Island, New York.

After dropping out of Boston University, Rosie began a career as a standup comedienne and actress, appearing in 1992 with Madonna and Tom Hanks in *A League of the Their Own*. Four years later, she was named host of daytime's syndicated *The Rosie O'Donnell Show*, where she developed a reputation as "The Queen of Nice"—and even faked a mad crush on the actor Tom Cruise. But Niagara Falls-sized cracks emerged in her nice gal reputation in 1999, when actor Tom Selleck appeared as Rosie's guest, a month after the Columbine shootings. Later, Tom said he'd been promised that the subject of gun control would not be raised during the interview. Rosie's spokesmouth denies this.

ROSIE: We're here with Tom Selleck who's a member of the NRA. Three months ago you joined the NRA.

TOM: I did. I actually joined to do an ad. Because, I've done a lot of consensus work for like the last seven to eight years and what disturbs me and disturbs a lot of Americans is the whole idea of politics nowadays which seems to be, "If you disagree with me, you must be evil" as opposed to "If you disagree with me, you must be stupid." That's very American. You know, the demonizing of a group like the NRA is very disturbing. . . . Reasonable people should disagree in this country; we should celebrate that, not consider it a threat.

ROSIE: Right, but I think that the reason that people are so extreme against the NRA is because the NRA has such a militant strength, especially a power in Washington to veto or to stronghold any sensible gun law. They have been against every sensible gun law, until yesterday, including trigger locks, so that children, which there are 500 a year that die, don't get killed.

TOM: I'm not a spokesman for the NRA. In fact, all I can tell you is, I was a member when I was a kid. I was a junior NRA member. I learned firearm safety. And from what I can see in the last three months, they don't do a lot of the stuff that you assume that they do.

ROSIE: I don't assume.

TOM: They are for trigger locks. The NRA is for a lot of things as long as they're voluntary.

ROSIE: They're against the registering of guns. We have to register cars. Why shouldn't we register guns so that when a crime is committed we can trace who has owned it?

TOM: You know I understand how you feel. This is a really contentious issue. Probably as contentious, and potentially as troubling, as the abortion issue in this country. All I can tell you is, rushes to pass legislation at a time of national crisis or mourning, I really don't think are proper. And more importantly, nothing in any of this legislation would have done anything to prevent that awful tragedy in Littleton. . . .

Guns were much more accessible forty years ago. A kid could walk into a pawnshop or a hardware store and buy a high capacity magazine weapon that could kill a lot of people and they didn't do it. The question we should be asking is, look, suicide is a tragedy. And it's a horrible thing. But thirty or forty years ago, particularly men, and even young men, when they were suicidal, they went, and unfortunately, blew their brains out. In today's world, someone who is suicidal sits home, nurses their grievance, develops a rage, and is just as suicidal but they take twenty people with them. There's something changed in our culture. That's not simple.

ROSIE: But you can't say that guns don't bear a responsibility. If the makers of the TEC-9 assault rifle—why wouldn't the NRA be against assault rifles? This is a gun that can shoot five bullets in a second. This is the gun that those boys brought into the school. Why the NRA wouldn't say as a matter of compromise, "We agree, assault weapons are not good?"

TOM: I'm not, I can't speak for the NRA.

ROSIE: But you're their spokesperson, Tom, so you have to be responsible for what they say.

TOM: But I'm not a spokesperson. I'm not a spokesperson for the NRA.

ROSIE: But if you put your name out and say, "I, Tom Selleck . . ."

TOM: (*visibly upset*) Don't put words in my mouth. I'm not a spokesperson. Remember how calm you said you'd be? Now you're questioning my humanity.

ROSIE: No, not your humanity. I think you're a very humane man. I'm saying that if you . . .

TOM: Let's just say that I disagree with you but I think you're being stupid.

The pair continued to joust, with Rosie interrupting Selleck, and the actor growing clearly angry. Mercifully, the clock wound down, and Rosie, finally, wrapped things up.

ROSIE: All right, well, this has not gone the way I had hoped it had gone. But I would like to thank you for appearing anyway, knowing we have differing views. I was happy that you decided to come on the show. And if you feel insulted by my questions, I apologize, because it was not a personal attack. It was meant to bring up the subject as it is in the consciousness of so many today. That was my intent. And if it was wrong, I apologize to you, on a personal level.

TOM: (*quietly*) It's your show, and you can talk about it after I leave, too.

Rosie's attempts to save the world through the absorption of children, a practice that's become a celebutard staple, hit a snag in 2000, after she completed a course to become a foster mom in Florida, where she keeps a home. Rosie took in a six-year-old boy, name unknown, but returned him to the foster care system after just two weeks because she felt he posed a danger to her family. It's a subject she discusses rarely.

Rosie quit her eponymous talk show in 2002, around the time she came out publicly as a lesbian, surprising no one, not even Tom Cruise. She announced she was in a relationship with Kelli Carpenter, a former dancer whom she "married" in San Francisco in 2004. The pair settled in Rockland County, New York, where they set out to raise three adopted kids—Parker Jaren, Chelsea Belle and Blake Christopher—plus daughter Vivienne Rose, to whom Kelli gave birth after being impregnated by a sperm donor. Rosie said she wanted to be a full-time mom. And she had a magazine to run. Well, maybe.

Once off the air, Rosie abandoned her Nice Queen schtick as quickly as one might abandon a heterosexual relationship. Called to fill in at the last minute as mistress of ceremonies for the Women in Film & Television's holiday luncheon at the Hilton in New York in 2002, Rosie proceeded to nuke her bridges. Facing women such as Frances McDormand, Alfre Woodard, Marlo Thomas and me, Rosie, done up in a lopsided butch haircut, said actress and shoplifter Winona Ryder "has been stealing sh*t for years" and should be locked up because "her last film sucked." She abused Michael Jackson for his extensive plastic reconstruction, and dismissed Joan Rivers as a "freak." As the audience fidgeted nervously, Rosie claimed to be simply telling the truth. She ended her bit by complaining that she could no longer park illegally in front of her kids' school, imitating a guard—"Your show's off the air, move your f*cking car."

The trial pitting magazine publisher Gruner + Jahr against Rosie O'Donnell unfolded with all the sobriety of a three-ring circus. G+J wanted to paint Rosie as poison in the editor's chair, and to this end it had an ace in the hole: the company put on the witness stand former colleague Cindy Spengler, who tearfully testified that Rosie once told her, cruelly, that people who lie "get sick and they get cancer." Spengler suffered from cancer.

The day Spengler took the stand, I got a behind-the-scenes peek into Planet Rosie. I sat in the courtroom, oohing and aahing over pictures of our daughters with Rosie's partner. Kelli turned out to be refreshingly humble, gracious and cute as she doted over her love interest, fetching Rosie sandwiches and soft drinks, and rubbing her back. Man, I could use a woman like that, and I'm straight.

Kelli told me that it was she who demanded Rosie apologize to Spengler, which Rosie did. In my column, I referred to Rosie's better half as her "wife"—which I worried might anger the couple with its stereotypical depiction of their roles. On the contrary, at trial's end Rosie stood on the courthouse steps and called Kelli her "wife." To adopt an expression I generally loathe—it is what it is.

Rosie may have been no peach to work with, but Gruner + Jahr was guilty of yanking Rosie's editorial control and hiring a safe, new editor at the exact moment she came out of the closet. In the end, State Supreme Court justice Ira Gammerman called it a tie—ruling that neither party was entitled to monetary damages. It was a victory for Rosie, who stood to lose millions, and she celebrated that night at a Manhattan pub. But as well-wishers hugged her, Rosie grew increasingly glum. "In a war," she told me, "a lot of innocent people get hurt."

Rosie next produced the ill-fated *Taboo* on Broadway about the early life of Boy George. It was a much better show than the critics gave her credit for. Still, it flopped. I'm not certain, but the bitter disappointment may have influenced Rosie's decision to lash out at an old friend.

In a piece she wrote for the *Advocate* about her marriage, Rosie segued into a rant about Martha Stewart's recent conviction on charges of obstruction of justice and lying to investigators. As far as I was concerned, it couldn't have happened to a more toxic shrew. It did not escape Rosie's notice that I was chief among Martha's haters. She wrote: "During my own trial, the smug *New York Post* columnist Andrea Peyser became my unlikely ally. That's because, at forty-two, I've been a professional entertainer for over two decades and I know how to work a room. I spoke to everyone during breaks. I chewed gum. I was me. I won Andrea over. Martha did not."

It stung. I never spoke to Rosie again.

Rosie would soon go off the reservation by waging a series of insane feuds, and expressing dumb theories about the terrorist attacks of September 11, 2001, that are so demonstrably loony and offensive, they should launch this micro-brained celebutard into a rubber room.

> *Rosie would soon go off the reservation by waging a series of insane feuds, and expressing dumb theories about the terrorist attacks of September 11, 2001, that are so demonstrably loony and offensive, they should launch this micro-brained celebutard into a rubber room.*

Rosie joined the cast of ABC's *The View* in September 2006, raising the show's ratings, but dealing it a blow from which it may never quite recover.

She took on *Live with Regis and Kelly* co-host Kelly Ripa, who objected in November 2006 when singer Clay Aiken put his hand over her mouth. "I just don't know where that hand's been, honey," said Kelly. Rosie retorted, "If that was a straight man . . . if that was a guy that she didn't question his sexuality, she would have said a different thing."

To her peril, she criticized Donald

Trump as a "snake-oil salesman," after he announced he was giving Miss USA Tara Conner a second chance at saving her crown. The small-town girl had run wild in the city, drinking while under age, and enjoying an open-mouthed kiss with Miss Teen USA Katie Blair, while hanging out with the likes of Ryan Seacrest.

"Left the first wife, had an affair. Left the second wife, had an affair—but he's the moral compass for twenty-year-olds in America!" Rosie opined.

Trump responded with a double-barrel barrage. He threatened to sue, derided Rosie's ballooning weight, and called her "an extremely unattractive person who doesn't understand the truth. . . . I think she's a terrible person. She has failed at everything she has done." He also promised to lure away Kelli.

IN LATE MARCH Rosie established her credentials as a card-carrying conspiracy whack job, suggesting that 7 World Trade Center, which was leveled in the September 11, 2001, terrorist attacks, had been purposefully imploded. Rosie said, on *The View*—"I do believe that it's the first time in history that fire has ever melted steel. I do believe that it defies physics that World Trade Center Tower 7—Building 7, which collapsed in on itself—it is impossible for a building to fall the way it fell without explosives being involved." Of course, she did not mention that the building housed New York City's emergency command bunker, and contained large fuel tanks throughout the building that fed generators by pressurized lines, as *Popular Mechanics* magazine wrote in its book, *Debunking 9/11 Myths*. But why let pesky facts get in the way of a good conspiracy?

In the coming weeks, Rosie proved incapable of shutting her lip. She became unglued in late April when she served as emcee of the Matrix Awards at the Waldorf Astoria, facing such media power houses as Rupert Murdoch, Senator Hillary Clinton, Joan Didion, Martha Stewart, Cindy Adams, seventeen high school scholarship winners, and myself.

Rosie repeatedly let loose the "F" bomb, and said she was sad when Donald Trump called her fat and disgusting because "it was always my dream to give an old, bald billionaire a boner." She concluded by grabbing her crotch and shouting "Eat me." Barbara Walters was observed lowering her head on the dais and covering her face with her hand. Two days later, ABC announced Rosie would leave the show when her contract ended in June.

Yet her ugly feud with token *View* conservative Elisabeth Hasselback proved to be the last gasp. It started May 17, when Rosie asked, stupidly, on air, "655,000 Iraqi civilians dead. Who are the terrorists? If you were in Iraq and another country, the United States, the richest in the world, invaded your country and killed 655,000 of your citizens, what would you call us?" What do you think Rosie meant?

The following Wednesday, Rosie complained her words had been "twisted." Rosie asked Elisabeth if she believed American soldiers were terrorists. Elisabeth hesitated. Then she sensibly asked Rosie to explain what she meant when she ranted about the troops. But Rosie ignored her.

A couple of days later, Rosie again shot her mouth at Elisabeth: "Because here's how it gets spun in the media," she said. "Rosie, big, fat, lesbian, loud Rosie, attacks innocent, pure Christian Elisabeth."

It was unfair. Elisabeth said, "I just don't understand why it's my fault if people spin words that you put out there or phrases that suggest things. And I gave you an opportunity two days ago to clarify the statement that got you in trouble on all those things."

"That got me in trouble?" Rosie asked sarcastically. "As a friend, you gave me the opportunity. That was very sweet of you. I was asking if you, who actually knows me, do you believe I think our troops are terrorists, Elisabeth? Do you believe that, yes or no?"

Elisabeth put her finger in the air. "Excuse me. Let me speak."

"You're going to doublespeak," said Rosie. "It's just a yes or a no."

It went on like this for ten grueling minutes, an eternity for television, as the show switched to a split screen, with each woman in a separate box.

"Every day since September I have told you that I support the troops," Rosie spat. "I asked you if you believed what the Republican pundits were saying. You said nothing, and that's cowardly."

"No, no, no!" Elisabeth shot back. "You will not call me a coward, because No. 1, I sit here every single day, open my heart and tell people exactly what I believe."

"So do I!"

"Do not call me a coward, Rosie."

"It was cowardly."

The next day, Rosie took a planned day off to celebrate Kelli's birthday. On Friday, March 25, she was gone from the show.

Barbara Walters wished her well.

And looked mighty relieved.

17

Curb Your Ignorance
LAURIE DAVID

*Sure, I have a big house, but I use it to gather hundreds
of people for eco-salons. That's not to justify the size of
it, but it does create opportunities to spread knowledge
and raise money for the greater environmental good.
Sure, I could always cut down on clothes and dry-cleaning,
but the point is not necessarily what more you could
do—we could all do more—the point is that we do our
part. And even with the house and clothes, I think I can
do, and am doing, my part.*

—Laurie David, to environmental website Grist.org, June 2004

LAURIE DAVID STANDS APART from the celebutards featured in this
volume because she is not an entertainer, politician, minister or
prison inmate. She is a wife. Or rather, she was the wife of a fabu-
lously rich and famous person, Seinfeld co-creator Larry David, an
achievement that has opened doors to her pet projects and opened
wallets in support of her obsession of choice—the urgent, imminent crisis of global warming. But those disciples inclined to enlist
in Laurie's army should be cautioned to do as Ms. David says, not
as she does. For while the erstwhile star wife is known to flip the
bird at those who drive gas-guzzling Hummers in Los Angeles from

behind the wheel of her Prius hybrid, she is then likely to fly, via Gulfstream jet, between her gargantuan, fuel-drinking California mansion and a second, humongous abode in Martha's Vineyard, Massachusetts. For this transgression, she is wholly unapologetic. It is in this hypocritical manner that Laurie David has grown into the living, breathing, dry-cleaning, embodiment of celebrity environmentalism.

She was born Laurie Ellen Lennard on March 22, 1958, in Long Island, New York. Her first brush with fame came when she started a career in New York City booking comedians for David Letterman. There, she met her future husband, Larry, an unknown who wanted five minutes of airtime. He was turned down. Only later would Larry David find fame, fortune and a "busty, shallow" wife—his words—through his wild success with *Seinfeld*, and for starring as a misanthropic comic with a fictionally tolerant spouse on HBO's *Curb Your Enthusiasm*. The Davids have produced two daughters.

Laurie's interest in global warming began as a hobby, then turned into an obsession, a religion and finally into a form of performance art in which the ability to spin seemingly contradictory ideas—SUVs bad, Gulfstream jets good—is paramount. She told the environmental website Grist.org that her environmental mania began at a breakfast with Robert F. Kennedy, Jr., son of the slain politician and an environmentalist himself.

"I sat down to breakfast with Bobby Kennedy and I got up from that table and I have not been the same since," she said. She was asked what Kennedy actually told her, but she couldn't remember a thing. "Nothing specific that I can remember. It was like ten years ago. I'm sure we talked about global warming and rivers and oceans and pollution and pesticides and toxins. The gist was that everybody should have the right to clean air and water the way they should have the right to affordable health care and racial equality. What's more basic than the right to health? One in four black kids in Harlem has asthma because of pollution—now that's a civil rights issue. It's an environmental-justice issue. A human issue."

Something happened in November 2004. Sorry, Laurie, but George W. Bush was re-elected president, soundly beating Democrat John Kerry. Laurie David described taking to her bed and crying for three days. If she neglected her two young daughters. I suppose she might justify the crying jag as serving the greater good. Because by the time she got out of bed, Laurie was more than an environmentalist. She was a crusader. A full-blown, fire-breathing celebutard.

Laurie set out to influence every man, woman, plant and child alive. She converted actors, starlets and studio heads in her circle at the salons she held in her monstrous, Tudor-style mansion in Los Angeles. It's a house she defends, despite its grotesque energy inefficiency, every bit as fiercely as she defends the planet.

"My philosophy about this stuff is, it's not all or nothing," she justified. "A lot of people have that attitude: 'So you drive a fuel-efficient car, what about your giant house? What about this, what about that?' I just got asked that on Paula Zahn and I was like, 'I'm not looking for perfection in any of this.' We're an imperfect people. But I really feel strongly that if everyone did one thing, we would be well on our way to a better planet. And I try to do more than one thing in my personal life.

"Of course, I'm obsessed with telling my kids, no long showers and don't run the water too much when you brush your teeth. I always use both sides of the paper for printing and faxing. I recycle obsessively."

Then came my absolutely favorite part of her rant: "And since I get a lot of clothes dry cleaned, I take a garment bag to the dry cleaner so that I don't waste the disposable plastic covers."

This prompted some perfectly logical questions—if dry cleaning is more harmful to the earth than plastic bags, why not dry clean fewer clothes? And why not live in a smaller house? She did not budge.

"Everybody has to strike their own balance between how they want to live and how they can reduce their impact. If the environmental movement wants to be mainstream, it has to lose its purer-than-thou, all-or-nothing attitude. It has to be pragmatic enough to bring everyone on board. If perfection is the measure, we will fail to appeal to anyone but the fringe." That is, the green tent should be big enough to hold every hypocritical Hollywood piglet. Even Laurie David.

She revealed to Britain's *Guardian* newspaper in 2006 that she forced Larry to use hard, recycled toilet paper—though she suspected he secretly filched some of the soft stuff from his daughter's bathroom that she brought home from friends' houses. She also admitted to banning Larry's golf shoes inside the house, because they might bear traces of pesticides. Finally, she limited Larry's showers to a minute and a half. Good thing Larry David is mostly bald, because that leaves no time for the application of conditioner.

Finally, she limited Larry's showers to a minute and a half. Good thing Larry David is mostly bald, because that leaves no time for the application of conditioner.

But Laurie also copped to being part of the problem, confessing that she's a member in good standing of the Lear jet liberal crowd.

"Yes, I take a private plane on holiday a couple of times a year, and I feel horribly guilty about it. I probably shouldn't do it. But the truth is, I'm not perfect. This is not about perfection. I don't expect anybody else to be perfect either. That's what hurts the environmental movement—holding people to a standard they cannot meet."

Um, I always thought burning excess fossil fuel is supposed to hurt the environment. But what do I know?

Finding detractors on the right is easy. Bernard Goldberg ranked her No. 82 in his 2005 book, *100 People Who Are Screwing Up America*. But Laurie David's jet-set life-style has brought condemnation even from her pals on the left. Ultra-liberal *Nation* columnist Eric Alterman, a friend, wrote in the *Atlantic*, "Laurie David, who dedicates herself to fighting for improved fuel-economy standards and reviles the owners of SUVs as terrorist enablers, gives herself a pass when it comes to chartering one of the most wasteful uses of fossil-based fuels imaginable: a private plane. (She's not just a limousine liberal; she's a Gulfstream liberal.)" Ouch.

New Republic writer Gregg Easterbrook estimated that "one cross-country flight in a Gulfstream is the same, in terms of Persian-Gulf dependence and greenhouse-gas emission, as if she drove a Hummer for an entire year." But remember—Laurie David screams at drivers of Hummers. Well, I guess eschewing that vehicle is like a fat person who pigs out on Twinkies, then tries to make amends for her gluttony by drinking Diet Coke.

For a long time, Larry David was forced to adapt. He stuck it out and provided financial support as she authored two books, produced a star-studded comedy special, *Earth to America!* for TBS, and an HBO documentary, *Too Hot Not to Handle*, as well as co-producing the Academy Award-winning, *An Inconvenient Truth* starring Laurie's fellow celebutard Al Gore.

He found the enthusiasm to speak these words at a fund-raiser for his wife's pet charity, the National Resources Defense Council, and reproduced them in his wife's 2006 book, *Stop Global Warming: The Solution is You!*: "Thirteen years ago I met a materialistic, narcissistic, superficial, bosomy woman from Long Island. She was the girl of my dreams. She read *People* magazine, watched hours of mindless television and shopped like there was no tomorrow. Finally I'd met someone as shallow as me. I was hopelessly in love. But then after a few, short months I began to sense that something had changed. She started peppering her conversation with words like 'ozone layer,' 'sustainable forestry' and 'toxic runoff.' " But what was not all too painfully obvious was that Larry David, the shallowest man in the world, had married an environmentalist."

The marriage came to an end in July 2007, when Laurie David filed for divorce after fourteen years of marriage, citing "irreconcilable differences." The differences reportedly may have had something to do with Martha's Vineyard resident Bart Thorpe, five years Laurie's junior. And a Republican. He was helping build a massive property for the Davids, and was frequently spotted in Laurie's company. His wife filed for divorce as well.

Thorpe was helping build for Laurie a new 25,000-square-foot house, bigger even than Al Gore's Tennessee spread, which was estimated to use twenty times as much energy as the average home in this country.

Laurie David has not addressed this hypocrisy. Except, when pressed, she told ABC that she'd try to fly commercial. Ick.

Asked by reporters for a reaction to his wife's abandonment, Larry passive-aggressively quipped, "I went home and turned all the lights on."

She's not done yet. In the fall of 2007, Laurie and co-author Cambria Gordon published *The Down-to-Earth Guide to Global Warming*. It's a children's book.

"Kids are the most optimistic human beings—they only see the future ahead of them and it's bright," David told *Publisher's Weekly*. "Kids also are the number one influence on their parents, so if you want to reach the parents, go to the kids."

There you have it. In her long-range plan to indoctrinate the public, Laurie David makes no apologies for scaring the stuffing out of children. It's all for the greater good!

Pass me a dry cleaning bag, Laurie. I fear I may be sick.

> *Asked by reporters for a reaction to his wife's abandonment, Larry passive-aggressively quipped, "I went home and turned all the lights on."*

18

Live from Celebutard Row

MUMIA ABU-JAMAL

Out of the many here assembled, it is the heart of he or she that I seek who looks at a life of vapid materialism, of capitalist excess, and finds it simply intolerable. It may be one hundred of you, or fifty, or even ten, or even one of you who makes that choice. I am here to honor and applaud that choice and to warn you that, though the suffering may indeed be great, it is nothing to the joy of doing the right thing.

—From convicted cop-killer Mumia Abu-Jamal's taped commencement address played at Evergreen State College in Olympia, Washington, June 11, 1999

Once again, this is an outrage and we have another marginal piece of allegedly higher education, which proves once again that you can get a better education in a public restroom than you can at one of these colleges.

—Rich Costello of the Fraternal Order of Police, on plans for Jamal to address Antioch College

MUMIA ABU-JAMAL—or Mumia, as his disciples affectionately refer to him—has the distinction of being the only celebutard in this volume convicted of first-degree murder. Others have done time, notably Paris Hilton (twenty-two days) and Lindsay Lohan (eighty-four minutes). But none except Mumia has been sentenced to death. If you don't mind, I'll just call him Abu-Jamal.

The Black Panther, radio reporter, and cab driver was ordered to die in 1982 for gunning down a Philadelphia police officer, Daniel Faulkner, a newlywed who was 12 days shy of his twenty-sixth birthday when he breathed his last. Abu-Jamal's death sentence was overturned in 2001, and transformed to a life prison term that he is currently serving in Pennsylvania, where he enjoys elite status as the prisoner with an energetic, star-studded fan club. He is routinely invited to address college commencements and municipal and civic organizations, for which he provides taped addresses. In 2003, he was named an honorary citizen of Paris, France—though I doubt he could get a table in a restaurant in downtown Philly. But to a specific swath of celebrity-worshiping America, Mumia Abu-Jamal has been anointed a rock star.

To understand Abu-Jamal's allure, realize that some inmates draw fan clubs of lonely women and confused men who are convinced the imprisoned are wrongly convicted. But Abu-Jamal has developed not just fans, but total fanatics who believe in him as fervently as they believe in building tremendous houses on California sand. It seems every Hollywood blowhard worth his bloated bank account has developed a thing for Abu-Jamal, from Susan Sarandon to Paul Newman, Whoopi Goldberg, Jason Alexander, and Oliver Stone. Tim Robbins and Mike Farrell took out a full-page ad in *The New York Times* advocating for a new trial, and the Beastie Boys played a concert to

It seems every Hollywood blowhard worth his bloated bank account has developed a thing for Abu-Jamal, from Susan Sarandon to Paul Newman, Whoopi Goldberg, Jason Alexander, and Oliver Stone.

raise money for Abu-Jamal's defense fund. Even former South African President and Nobel Peace prize laureate Nelson Mandela, who served twenty-seven years in his country's Robben Island prison, has jumped on the Free Mumia bandwagon, evidently making the common mistake of confusing the convicted celebutard with a persecuted individual.

If his fans had their way, Mumia Abu-Jamal would be free to roam the streets tomorrow. I recommend he take up residence in Susan Sarandon and Tim Robbins' guest room.

The crime for which Jamal received the maximum penalty is fairly straightforward: At around 3:51 A.M. on December 9, 1981, police officer Daniel Faulkner routinely stopped a car driven by Abu-Jamal's brother, William Cook, on a Philadelphia street. As he handcuffed Cook and awaited backup, Mumia Abu-Jamal emerged from a taxi parked across the street. According to testimony at his trial, confirmed by his conviction and upheld by no less an authority than the United States Supreme Court, it all ended after Jamal pulled out a .38-caliber revolver and shot Faulkner in the back. The officer got off a shot that hit Abu-Jamal in the chest. But the wounded assailant—and Abu-Jamal's fans strenuously contend it could have been someone else—came back and emptied his gun in Faulkner's head. Despite his injuries, Abu-Jamal lived; Faulkner did not.

Those interested in truth and justice might call this an open-and-shut case. For one thing, a .38 that Abu-Jamal had owned since 1979 was found nearby, with five spent cartridges in the cylinder. But legions of the Hollywood upper crust, as well as enthusiastic supporters regularly churned out by mainly West Coast universities, have flocked to Jamal's aid. To the Free Mumia brigade, his conviction and sentence are a grave miscarriage of justice. To Faulkner's widow, Maureen, it has been more than a quarter century of uninterrupted hell. Because those who want Abu-Jamal to walk are not terribly interested in who killed Daniel Faulkner. Mumiamites contend that a black man in America cannot find justice under any circumstances. In other words, even if Abu-Jamal did the crime, he should be let go.

He was born Wesley Cook on April 24, 1954, and was given the name Mumia in 1968 by his high school teacher who hailed from Kenya. He added Abu-Jamal, which means "father of Jamal," after the birth of his son, Jamal, from his first wife in 1971.

He was charged with assault for trying to disrupt a George Wallace for President rally in 1968, a credential that doubtless curries great favor with the Hollywood set. The next year he helped form the Philadelphia chapter of the Black Panther Party, dropping out of high school and marrying three times. He earned his high-school equivalency diploma, the last formal education Abu-Jamal ever received. He worked various, mostly brief, stints at local radio stations, in which Abu-Jamal espoused the propaganda of radical groups with which he was affiliated, especially the anti-government, anti-technology organization, MOVE. Abu-Jamal was also active in the Marijuana Users Association of America.

After Faulkner was murdered in 1981, Abu-Jamal tried to represent himself at trial, but was removed after he refused to accept the judge's rulings on points of law. He was so disruptive, the judge kicked him out of the courtroom repeatedly. When things finally got rolling, the prosecution presented four eyewitnesses to the crime: a prostitute, a motorist, a pedestrian and an unlicensed cab driver on parole for arson. Who else would be wandering the streets at 4:00 A.M.? Needless to say, the testimony has been discredited by Abu-Jamal's people.

He did not testify in his own defense, declaring years later, "At my trial I was denied the right to defend myself. I had no confidence in my court-appointed attorney, who never even asked me what happened the night I was shot and the police officer was killed; and I was excluded from at least half the trial. Since I was denied all my rights at my trial I did not testify. I would not be used to make it look like I had a fair trial."

He was tried. He was convicted. The entire, ugly episode appeared over. In reality, Mumia Abu-Jamal was just getting warmed up.

It was only after Abu-Jamal was behind bars that he truly began to live. Not terribly successful as a journalist while on the outside, once on the inside he became a world-renowned author and speaker, producing such works as *Live From Death Row*, a collection of commentaries published in 1995 by Addison-Wesley, who paid Abu-Jamal a $30,000 advance. This caused Faulkner's widow, Maureen, to claim that the sum, which went to Abu-Jamal's defense fund and his family, defied Pennsylvania's Son of Sam law that bars criminals from profiting from crime. One day, the dead man's widow hired an airplane to buzz company headquarters with a banner affixed to the rear that read, "Addison-Wesley Supports Cop Killer."

But even the appellation "cop killer" has angered some of Abu-Jamal's fans, who insist the term makes it look as if he habitually kills police officers, while he's only been convicted of killing a single cop.

Abu-Jamal appears amused by such sideshows, having found fame, influence and a seat high atop the celebustocracy at the center of a movement dedicated to toppling the American justice system. His disciples have gone so far as to claim the authorities found a way to frame Abu-Jamal for having been a Black Panther. Such theories, frankly, give the man more importance than he ever enjoyed when he was a mere cab driver, struggling reporter, and dedicated pot smoker.

Those who believe the ivory tower is fuzzy-headed and out of touch were handed ample ammunition in June 1999, when Evergreen State College, a four-year liberal arts institution in Olympia, Washington, extended Abu-Jamal an invitation to provide a commencement address.

Washington Governor Gary Locke canceled his scheduled appearance at the college in protest. House majority leader Tom DeLay declared Abu-Jamal was selected by "twisted radicals" who "perverted their vocation to better mankind through teaching." Lynne Abraham, who prosecuted Abu-Jamal in 1982, said, "To dignify a graduation ceremony with the words of a convicted killer is an obscenity."

But college president Jane Jervis was determined to put her college on the map, insisting that Abu-Jamal served "to galvanize an international conversation about the death penalty, the disproportionate number of blacks on death row, and the relationship between poverty and the criminal justice system." Not a mention about the wisdom of giving a platform to a convicted murderer.

In the end, Abu-Jamal provided a taped address. He spoke for thirteen minutes.

To this day, Abu-Jamal has never spoken about the case for which he was convicted, except to declare his innocence. His brother, William, also has not talked about what happened the fateful night of December 9, 1981, except to say that neither he nor his brother shot Officer Faulkner.

But who did?

In 1999, *Vanity Fair* magazine published a lengthy story in which an Abu-Jamal supporter, Phillip Bloch, claimed his one-time idol confessed to murdering the police officer. Bloch said that during a prison visit in 1992, he asked Abu-Jamal if he regretted killing Daniel Faulkner. Abu-Jamal replied simply, "Yes." Bloch said he spoke out because he was concerned about the intense vilification of the dead man. The vilification continues today.

Abu-Jamal's fans went crazy. They set out to debunk the story and discredit Bloch, and also took off on a similar piece aired by ABC TV's *20/20*. Abu-Jamal himself said cryptically, "A lie is a lie, whether made today or ten years later." In a fit of snark, he also thanked *Vanity Fair* for keeping alive the controversy over his case.

Maureen Faulkner's voice has largely been mute over the years. Except for weak stunts like hiring a plane to protest the publication of Abu-Jamal's book, she has been violently out shouted by the Mumiaphiles, and badly outspent. However, in 2007 a small publisher printed her memoir, written with conservative talk show host

> *Maureen Faulkner has been sentenced to live with a pain that will continue as long as Abu-Jamal's Celebutard Nation continues its assault on her husband's memory.*

Michael Smerconish, *Murdered by Mumia: A Life Sentence of Loss, Pain and Injustice*. True to form, pro-Abu-Jamal protesters assembled outside NBC's *Today* show during Mrs. Faulkner's appearance to promote the book, demanding equal time. They didn't get it.

Maureen Faulkner has been sentenced to live with a pain that will continue as long as Abu-Jamal's Celebutard Nation continues its assault on her husband's memory. Her ache will endure as long as the stars whip up a gullible public. Her agony will live, as long as Abu-Jamal speaks, publishes and breathes.

I'm afraid she will suffer for a long time to come.

19

Sheehan Is Unbelieving

CINDY SHEEHAN

On September 11, 3,000 Americans were killed. So does that make George Bush ten times the bigger terrorist than Osama bin Laden?
　　—Cindy Sheehan, January 2006

THIS HARD-CORE CELEBUTARD achieved fame not for being particularly smart, colorful, gorgeous or talented, but for being a mom, a role that bestows on her instant credibility and, her fans hope, untouchability. For Sheehan lost her son in Iraq.

Sheehan, born Cindy Lee Miller on July 10, 1957, has offered herself up as the face of the anti–Iraq War movement, becoming the instant darling of not only the radical left, but of various deep-thinking celebrities, from Michael Moore to Susan Sarandon. In August 2005, this woman from northern California won international exposure when she pitched her tent outside President George W. Bush's ranch near Crawford, Texas, creating Camp Casey after her son, an Army specialist who died in 2004 at age twenty-four.

Sheehan's goal was to confront the president, with whom she'd talked once before. But after a month in which she entertained some 1,500 people, including movie stars and members of Congress, Sheehan confessed she was glad Bush didn't stop by—it would have stalled the glorious attention coming her way.

The world's most famous mom is like a movie screen onto which followers project whatever it is they want to see. In truth, Cindy Sheehan is not the brightest bulb to grace the chandelier. That has not stopped a fascinated media mob from asking her to state opinions on issues for which she has no business spouting, from the attacks on the World Trade Center—which she suspects came down in a controlled demolition—to opining that too much coverage was wasted on the "little wind" generated by Hurricane Rita.

During Sheehan's initial encampment at Camp Casey, her husband of twenty-eight years, Patrick, filed for divorce. But while Cindy Sheehan has deemed it appropriate to drag the president's family into her activism—"If it's such a noble cause, why aren't his daughters over there?"—she has bristled when asked if her new career as a celebrity-friendly symbol drove away her spouse. She finally admitted that her husband couldn't handle the ferocity of her quest, to which she appears to have grown addicted. She also cut ties with her in-laws because they "voted for the person who killed their grandson."

But if Sheehan's ardent supporters, which include David Letterman, like to see her face, they aren't always crazy about what comes out of it.

She accused the media of giving too much coverage to Hurricane Rita, instead of Cindy Sheehan, in her Daily Kos diary in September 2005. "I am watching [CNN] and it is 100 percent Rita . . . even though it is a little wind and a little rain."

And in March 2005, an e-mail purportedly from Sheehan was forwarded to ABC's *Nightline* that said her son "joined the Army to protect America, not Israel." Sheehan has insisted the e-mail was altered to make her look bad. Yet two other people have stepped forward saying the wording was consistent with that in e-mails sent directly by Sheehan.

I guess being a world-class activist makes you an expert on all things. In an interview on Alex Jones' radio show, she lent support to the mad theory that the World Trade Center was not brought down by planes. "I'm not an expert and I haven't had time to research it," she said, "but it does look to me like a controlled demolition from a very amateur eye."

I don't like to question a woman's patriotism. Well, not usually. But in January 2006, Cindy Sheehan embraced America-hating Venezuelan president Hugo Chavez at the sixth annual World Social Forum in Caracas. The world press steered clear of the event, hosted by a dictator known the world over for imprisoning critics, wet-kissing terrorists, and shutting down the free press.

And she calls Bush a terrorist.

Teflon Mom was asked by MSNBC's *Hardball* fill-in host Norah O'Donnell if she would rather live in Venezuela under Chavez. You could hear the peace movement—well, all except butcher-hugger Sean Penn—cringe at her reply.

"Yes, Hugo Chavez is not a dictator like you introduced him," she replied stupidly. "He's been democratically elected eight times. He is not anti-American, he has helped the poor people of America . . ."

Sheehan said she was going on a two-month hunger strike to protest the war. By the way, she survived.

> *Sheehan said she was going on a two-month hunger strike to protest the war. By the way, she survived.*

In May 2007, Sheehan suspended her quest. "I am going to take whatever I have left and go home. I am going to go home and be a mother to my surviving children and try to regain some of what I have lost."

But Cindy shortly neglected her knitting.

Just when you thought she couldn't get any loopier, Sheehan transformed from peace activist into full-blown defender of (alleged) killers. She popped up in Egypt in February 2008 at a protest in which she asked the country's first lady, Suzanne Mubarak, to stop a military trial against accused Islamic terrorists, money launderers and assorted evil guys.

"I am here to protest the trial of civilians in front of a military tribunal as this is a violation to international law. As a mother of a son who was killed in the war, I presented a letter to Ms. Suzanne Mubarak to realize how those women and children are suffering." And they'll suffer even more, Cindy, if the bad guys go free.

Some women just need attention, I guess. But really, Cindy, find a hobby.

20

Attack of the Bloviator
ALEC BALDWIN

I believe that what happened in 2000 did as much
damage to the pillars of democracy as terrorists did
to the pillars of commerce in New York City.

—Baldwin compares the September 11, 2001, terror attacks to the
election, Florida A&M University, Tallahassee, Florida, 2002

THE NEW YORK POST Page Six gossip column calls Alec Baldwin "The Bloviator" for his loud and unasked-for ruminations on everything from terrorism, which he compares to the disappointing results of the 2000 election, to his daughter, whom he compares to a "pig." Perhaps Page Six is too kind.

Born Alexander Rae Baldwin III on April 3, 1958, in Massapequa, New York, Baldwin is the son of Carol and Alexander Rae Baldwin Jr., a high school teacher. He graduated from New York University with a Bachelor of Fine Arts degree. Alec Baldwin, as he was eventually known, is the oldest and most celebrated of the four acting Baldwin brothers, famed for his roles in movies (*The Hunt for Red October*) and television (*30 Rock*). But Baldwin told *The New York Times* in October 2006 that he wants to run for governor of New York, commenting about that other acting governor, Arnold

Schwarzenegger of California, "I'm Tocqueville compared to Schwarzenegger."

Baldwin tested his political chops, his temper and his sanity, when he went cuckoo on *Late Night with Conan O'Brien* eight days before President Bill Clinton was to be impeached in 1998, declaring:

"If we were in another country . . . we would stone [Republican Representative] Henry Hyde to death and we would go to their homes and kill their wives and their children. We would kill their families."

It wasn't until later, when Baldwin went after his own daughter in a terrifying rage, that we learned the true extent of his scariness. In what's become a familiar pattern of hit and retreat, Baldwin apologized for the remarks about Hyde.

NBC promised never to re-air the show.

Baldwin's then-wife, actress Kim Basinger, told a German magazine, *Focus*, in 2000 that Baldwin promised to leave the United States if George W. Bush beat Al Gore for the White House. When that happened and Baldwin remained stateside, the actor at first denied Basinger had talked to the magazine, but later flip-flopped and acknowledged that she did. Baldwin then changed his comment to suggest he would not leave the country now.

"I think my exact comment was that if Bush won it would be a good time to leave the United States. I'm not necessarily going to leave the United States." Too bad.

In a piece written for the online *Huffington Post* in 2006, Baldwin called Vice President Dick Cheney a "terrorist."

"He terrorized our enemies abroad and innocent citizens here at home indiscriminately."

He wound up taking it back, and replacing the statement with one in which he said Cheney is "a lying, thieving oil whore and a murderer of the U.S. Constitution." He's also called President Bush a "trust fund puppet" and Cheney a "constitution hating sociopath." Glad we cleared that up.

Baldwin outdid himself when he compared the 2000 presidential election to the September 11, 2001, terror attacks to a college audience in Tallahassee, Florida.

"I know that's a harsh thing to say, perhaps, but I believe that what happened in 2000 did as much damage to the pillars of democracy as terrorists did to the pillars of commerce in New York City."

A man who feels free to call an elected official a "terrorist," and to downplay a series of murderous attacks on New York (he didn't mention the Pentagon or Pennsylvania) as wreaking damage only to "the pillars of commerce" might consider being careful with his tongue. Otherwise, some might suspect he harbors secret savage tendencies.

Need proof? Here is a transcript of a voice mail Alec Baldwin left in April 2007 for his eleven-year-old daughter, Ireland, at the California home of his ex-wife Kim Basinger.

BALDWIN: Hey, I want to tell you something, okay? And I want to leave a message for you right now. 'Cause again, it's 10:30 here in New York on a Wednesday, and once again I've made an ass of myself trying to get to a phone to call you at a specific time. When the time comes for me to make the phone call, I stop whatever I'm doing and I go and I make that phone call. At eleven o'clock in the morning in New York and if you don't pick up the phone at ten o'clock at night. And you don't even have the f*cking phone turned on. I want you to know something, okay?

I'm tired of playing this game with you. I'm leaving this message with you to tell you you have insulted me for the last time. You have insulted me. You don't have the brains or the decency as a human being. I don't give a damn that you're twelve years old, or eleven years old, or that you're a child, or that your mother is a thoughtless pain in the ass who doesn't care about what you do as far as I'm concerned. You have humiliated me for the last time with this phone.

And when I come out there next week, I'm going to fly out there for the day just to straighten you out on this issue. I'm going to let you know just how disappointed in you I am and how angry I am with you that you've done this to me again. You've made me feel like sh*t and you've made me feel like a fool over and over and over again. And this crap you pull on me with this f*cking phone situation that you would never dream of doing to your mother and you do it to me constantly and over and over again. I am going to get on a plane and I am going to come out there for the day and I am going to straighten your ass out when I see you.

Do you understand me? I'm going to really make sure you get it. Then I'm going to get on a plane and I'm going to turn around and come home. So you'd better be ready Friday the twentieth to meet with me. So I'm going to let you know just how I feel about what a rude little pig you really are. You are a rude, thoughtless little pig, okay?

He was caught being Alec Baldwin. So naturally, he blamed someone else, namely Basinger, for leaking the tape to the media in the middle of a nasty custody battle, and causing him to lose all self control. Basinger denies publicizing the tape.

A spokesperson for the actor released a statement that said, "In the best interest of the child, Alec will do what the mother is pathologically incapable of doing . . . keeping his mouth shut and obeying the court order. The mother and her lawyer leaked this sealed material in violation of a court order. Although Alec acknowledges that he should have used different language in parenting his child"—I'll say—"everyone who knows him privately knows what he has been put through for the past six years."

Thankfully, Baldwin never had a chance with his daughter to "straighten you out." A superior court commissioner temporarily suspended Baldwin's visitation rights.

As if on cue, Baldwin temporarily stopped blaming Basinger. He publicly apologized to his little girl, whose exact age he couldn't quite put his finger on. Then he started bashing Basinger again, saying his diatribe was aimed at the wrong female.

He was not through. In 2008, he released a book that gives—are you ready?—advice to divorcing dads.

He publicly apologized to his little girl, whose exact age he couldn't quite put his finger on.

A word of advice to Alec Baldwin: When fighting for custody, refrain from calling your child any type of farm animal. I wish someone would straighten this guy out.

21

Wicked Witch of the West Wing
HILLARY CLINTON

He ran a gas station down in St. Louis . . . No, Mahatma
Gandhi was a great leader of the twentieth century.

> —Hillary Clinton joking about the Indian leader at a St. Louis
> fund-raiser, January 2004

We're going to take things away from you on behalf of
the common good.

> —Hillary warns well-to-do Democrats that federal tax cuts
> will end, San Francisco, June 2004

I could hardly breathe. Gulping for air, I started crying
and yelling at him, "What do you mean? What are you
saying? Why did you do this to me?"

> —Confronting Bill's infidelity in her 2003 memoir, *Living History*

HILLARY HAS THE HONOR of being the first celebutard to run for
president of the United States. One man morphed into celebutardom after losing the White House (Al Gore), and another achieved
celebutard status after spending time in the Oval Office (Jimmy
Carter). But Hillary stands as the only person, man or woman, who

would shamelessly ride her brush with fame (marriage to Bill Clinton) and humiliation (Monica Lewinsky) nearly to the top role in politics even before the ink was dry on her Official Celebutard certificate. Don't underestimate her.

You'll notice that I call her Hillary. Not Hillary Rodham, as she was known early in her marriage, not Hillary Rodham Clinton, as she grudgingly renamed herself during her irritating Political Wife phase, and not even Hillary Clinton, as she sheepishly defined herself during the period in which she publicly licked her wounds and played stand-by-your-man.

For a time, I wickedly labeled her "Monica Lewinsky's ex-boyfriend's wife," a phrase I saw reproduced on a bumper sticker.

She is Hillary, a singular creature. Some women in her position would take up hobbies. Others would file for divorce or resort to physical violence. But Hillary's self control borders on science fiction. She has worked too hard, studied too intensely, and endured embarrassments that would have felled a lesser creature—all in a fiercely focused quest to get to a place where she might stand on her own, wield incredible power, and most importantly, get the last laugh.

Hillary Diane Rodham was born October 26, 1947, in Chicago, Illinois, the daughter of Hugh Rodham, who ran a successful textile business, and Dorothy, a homemaker. She has two younger brothers.

HILLARY ENTERED COLLEGE AS, of all things, a Young Republican, but was rapidly radicalized by her commitment to civil-rights struggles and her opposition to the Vietnam War. In 1969, as she received her bachelor's degree in political science, Wellesley College made her the first student in history to deliver a commencement address. It would be Hillary's ticket to fame, leading to a seven-minute standing ovation and a profile in *Life* magazine. Years later, the speaker who preceded Hillary to the podium, a mild-mannered, Republican African-American Senator from Massachusetts—the only black man in the Senate—Edward Brooke, reflected on serving as the road kill beneath Hillary's loafers.

Before Hillary stood up, Brooke addressed the students about political dissent. (Coincidentally, Brooke was Barbara Walters' married lover in the '70s, she revealed in her 2008 memoir, launching a veritable celebutard daisy chain.) He ended his Wellesley remarks by mentioning that the national poverty rate, which stood at 22 percent in 1959, had fallen to 13.3 percent a decade later. He interpreted that statistic as meaning that society cares about people, but needs to do more. He never saw the freight train coming.

HILLARY TOOK the stage with both guns blazing. She "was not rude but her tone was strident," Brooke wrote in his 2007 memoir, *Bridging the Divide*. "She challenged my comment as if we were in a debate."

Here's what she said: "What does it mean to hear that 13.3 percent of the people in this country are below the poverty line? That's a percentage. We're not interested in social reconstruction; it's human reconstruction. How can we talk about percentages and trends?"

Thirty-eight years later Brooke, still smarting, concluded, "I think that no matter who the commencement speaker had been that day, or what he or she had said, Hillary Rodham planned to use the situation to her advantage." He was all the more stunned because Hillary had volunteered for his 1966 Senate campaign. For Hillary, loyalty would not come naturally.

For years, the White House put Hillary's senior thesis under lock and key, keeping critics awake at night. She wrote it on union organizer Saul Alinsky, who's been called a Communist. The thesis was dubbed the "Rosetta Stone" which would provide answers to Hillary's radical ways. Why was the White House hiding it?

The fuss, however, was lifted in 2001, after the Clintons left office and the paper was made available to anyone who could slog through it. Hillary was stupid to have concealed a rather pedestrian paper, written in formal academic language, in which she agrees with Alinsky that the poor are powerless, but writes that the man may actually have hurt unfortunate souls by delaying their entry into the moneyed classes. Hillary got an "A" on the paper. Critics lost their Rosetta.

It was at Yale Law School that the committed feminist began dating the man who would determine her personal and professional future, that charming rascal from Arkansas, Bill Clinton. Several times, she turned down offers of marriage, afraid that hitching her wagon to his would subsume her identity.

She served as a member of the impeachment inquiry staff in Washington, D.C., whose work drove President Richard M. Nixon to resign from office in 1974 before, ol' Bill wore her down.

The pair wed in 1975, settling down in Arkansas. Hillary kept her maiden name, something that upset both her and Bill's mother. She became partner in the Rose Law firm, which concentrated within its walls all the power and influence you can squeeze into Arkansas. The Clintons' perennial good fortune, and their gleeful unwillingness to explain why they were so blessed, would from that day forward go hand-in-hand, like country music, dogs and infidelity.

In 1980, daughter Chelsea was born.

As Hillary moved up the food chain as a Southern player, Bill made his run at political power, getting elected state attorney general, then governor. It was around this time, the early 1980s, that Hillary, ever-grudgingly, sometimes started using the name "Clinton."

Before Bill was elected president, the bimbos started erupting. First to appear was Gennifer Flowers, an Arkansas lounge singer who held a press conference announcing a twelve-year affair with the governor. With the benefit of hindsight, today we may parse Bill Clinton's denial, which he made during a 1992 post-Super Bowl appearance with Hillary on *60 Minutes*.

STEVE KROFT: She [Flowers] is alleging and has described in some detail in the supermarket tabloid what she calls a twelve-year affair with you.

BILL CLINTON: That allegation is false.

He was telling the truth, Clintonian style. Flowers later admitted that her affair with Clinton did not carry on as long as she initially claimed. But in 1992 Kroft, and the rest of America, had no experience with a man who would one day face the nation on television and declare, "I did not have sexual relations with that woman"—and mean that oral sex didn't count. Apparently, neither did the unorthodox use of a cigar.

> HILLARY CLINTON: You know, I'm not sitting here—some little woman standing by my man like Tammy Wynette. I'm sitting here because I love him, and I respect him, and I honor what he's been through and what we've been through together. And you know, if that's not enough for people, then heck, don't vote for him.

She also suggested—in what would become a familiar defense—that Flowers was a complete wacko. It was not the last time the little woman would bail out her miserable husband. And not the first time she ran roughshod over the reputation of someone who got in her way.

Was this payback? Bill Clinton campaigned for president on the promise of "two for the price of one," meaning Hillary would be in charge, too. On November 3, 1992, he was elected the forty-second president of the United States. Hillary, making good on the co-president threat, took an office in the West Wing of the White House, not the east, where First Ladies normally preside. From the start, it was a disaster.

Fresh from the election, Bill put his wife in charge of concocting a national health-care plan. Why an unelected First Lady should be handed such awesome responsibility was a question he preferred not to address. Hillary attempted to push down America's throat a monster program that smacked of the old Soviet Union. She operated secretively, claiming, like your mother, to know what's best.

Critics, shut out of the planning, their views marginalized by

Hillary, felt the health care program was too expensive, too big, too centrally controlled. It was abandoned before reaching a vote in Congress. Hillary's first all-out debacle is considered a chief reason Republicans gained fifty-three seats in the House and seven in the Senate during the 1994 mid-term elections. When it was over, Hillary licked her wounds by talking to the spirit of Eleanor Roosevelt, another politically active First Lady whom she felt was also misunderstood. For the first time, people started whispering that Hillary might be a loon.

If Bill Clinton was a likeable character, distrust, even hatred, stuck to Hillary like Velcro. She was dubbed "Lady Macbeth," the emasculating power behind the throne. In many ways, the title proved accurate.

The Clinton years were scarred by scandals inevitably tagged by the suffix "gate"—echoes of "Watergate"—and Hillary was front and center for every one. "Whitewatergate" questioned Hillary's conflict of interest in an Arkansas land deal that lost people millions. In "Travelgate," Hillary was accused of firing the entire White House travel office in order to give business to friends in Arkansas. Vince Foster's 1993 suicide to this day raises questions about whether Hillary ordered that potentially damaging files related to the Whitewater scandal be removed from Foster's office. What did he know that was worth dying for?

In "Filegate," Hillary was accused of gathering hundreds of FBI background reports on former Republican White House employees. Even a $1,000 investment in cattle futures made while in Arkansas, which generated an eye-popping $100,000 profit, came back to bite her—was the profit on the deal really a bribe?

In 1996, world-renowned physician Dr. Burton Lee told me that at the dawn of the Clinton administration he was fired from the White House medical office after he asked to see President Clinton's health records. "There isn't any question in my mind that the person who fired me was Hillary," Lee told me.

Her fingerprints were everywhere, but they vanished like writing in the sand. When the Independent Counsel issued final reports on various Clinton scandals in 2000, they contained insufficient evidence against Hillary.

The mark of Hillary would also vanish from the case that would mark the First Lady's biggest disgrace, as well as her greatest opportunity: the Monica Lewinsky Mess.

But before Monica, there was Paula Jones.

In 1994, Jones charged that three years earlier, then-Governor Clinton lured her into a hotel room with the help of a state trooper—launching yet another scandal dubbed "Troopergate." She said he exposed his penis and asked for sex. She turned him down.

This revelation led Clinton strategist James Carville to dismiss her with, "Drag $100 bills through trailer parks, there's no telling what you'll find."

Jones, crude and unpolished, was laughed at. Her husband divorced her. Her lawsuit was dismissed. But she won vindication of a sort after Clinton settled with her for $850,000, money she used for plastic surgery. The floodgates were open.

In 1998, Juanita Broaddrick accused Bill Clinton of raping her two decades earlier. Kathleen Willey accused him of putting her hand on his penis and grabbing her breast. Neither claim ended with charges, but they made for good headlines—Hide the kids! A sitting president was running amok! It would have spelled death to another marriage. But Bill and Hillary hunkered down together, and fought the accusations like professional hit men. Hillary was not giving up her perch, a heartbeat from power, for all the bimbos in the world.

But try as they might to kill it, the Jones affair would not die. And it spawned the event that would linger over his presidency, and, ironically, become the launching pad for Hillary's political career. Clinton perjured himself in the Jones case. He denied, under oath, that he had sex with yet another woman, Monica Lewinsky, the intern who would soon haunt his every waking minute, and torture his long and sleepless nights.

First came the denials.

"I did not have sexual relations with that woman, Miss Lewinsky," Bill Clinton swore to the nation, live on TV, in 1998. It was a shot heard 'round the world.

"It is this vast right-wing conspiracy that has been conspiring against my husband since the day he announced for president," Hillary fired off on the *Today* show.

IT HAS BEEN widely reported—and flatly denied by Hillary's scandal lawyer, David Kendall—that disgraced Hollywood "investigator to the stars" Anthony Pellicano (long before he was convicted in 2008 of racketeering, wiretapping, and running a criminal enterprise) was brought in by Hillary in 1992 to analyze and discredit sexually explicit tape recordings between Bill Clinton and Gennifer Flowers.

WAS HE INVOLVED? Mary Matalin, political director for the first President Bush's re-election campaign, said on her syndicated radio show in 1997: "I got the letters from Pellicano to [women linked to Clinton] intimidating them. I had tapes of the conversations from Pellicano to the women. I got handwritten letters from the women. I got one letter from one of the women's dads, saying, 'This is so horrible. Here's what they're going to do to us.' "

One wonders how Monica Lewinsky's former Beverly Hills High School drama teacher and lover, Andy Bleiler, miraculously appeared on his Oregon porch one day in the midst of scandal, alongside his miserable-looking wife. As if reading from the Clintons' script, he dubbed Monica a stalker.

Blieiler's lawyer famously quoted a scheming Lewinsky as having her sights set on servicing Bill Clinton in any way possible.

"I'm going to go to Washington to get my presidential knee pads," quoth Lewinsky.

I asked Pellicano in 1998 if he had a hand in dredging up Bleiler. He would not confirm or deny.

He did say, somewhat oddly, "You're a smart girl. No comment."

BUT IT ALL UNRAVELED, like the seams on the blue semen-stained dress that Lewinsky carefully put away.

Unfortunately for Bill (or maybe not) Monica Lewinsky had a big mouth. She blabbed of the affair in conversations surreptitiously tape recorded by White House staffer Linda Tripp, who hoped to write a book.

> *Unfortunately for Bill (or maybe not) Monica Lewinsky had a big mouth.*

Bill gave unfortunate testimony to a Grand Jury, in which he explained he was telling the truth when he said he isn't sexing up a lowly intern.

"It depends on what the meaning of the word 'is' is," he said. It should be etched on his tombstone.

Independent Counsel Kenneth Starr had been looking to nail the Clintons for financial malfeasance related to Whitewater. But Clinton was prosecuted for lying about Monica. That's right, the president of the United States, leader of the free world, was impeached for receiving a blow job.

Bill Clinton became only the second president in history to be impeached, charged with perjury and obstruction of justice. (The Senate acquitted him in 1999, as it did Andrew Johnson 131 years earlier.)

For Hillary, life began here. She was transformed into the sympathetic, wounded party. In her memoir, *Living History*, Hillary shrieked with raw emotion at Bill, whom she exiled to sleep on the couch. The histrionics seemed unlikely from a woman so controlled. But the description polled well with her core supporters: women.

For the Cuckolded First Wife, a career was born.

I suspect that Hillary has always held lofty political ambitions that she buried when she wed an ambitious, natural politician. A man who makes charming the pants (literally) off the public look so effortless, in comparison to Hillary's painstaking hard work. But with Bill out of the White House and Chelsea grown, she had little to absorb her day. So ahead of the 2000 election, Hillary packed up Bill, bought a house in Chappaqua, New York, and ran as a Democrat for the Senate. Never mind that she sought to represent a state in which she'd never before lived.

If one wants to shed the title of "carpetbagger" in New York, she'd better prove her affinity to the Jewish people. To that end, a funny story appeared in the *Forward* newspaper in 1999, revealing that Hillary's grandmother, Della Murray, had in the 1930s married a Russian-born Jew with the authentic name Max Rosenberg. Why Hillary's distant Jewish connection was unearthed at this critical moment was never revealed, nor was the identity of the person who planted the story. Who knew?

During her campaign, Hillary visited every last one of New York's sixty-two counties, most of them rural and majority Republican—places that hadn't seen a politician in, well, ever. Hillary nonetheless rolled into towns and sat in the auditorium, the living room, the barn, nodding her head until I feared it would fall off, while listening to the people's gripes and groans about a collapsing upstate economy. Hillary outclassed her forgettable opponent, Republican Representative Rick Lazio, in November 2000, winning by a margin of 55 to 43 percent. Six years later, she won re-election against Republican John Spencer, 67 to 31 percent.

I got a rare—and purely accidental—up close insight into the Clintons' unholy union during the 2004 Democratic convention in Boston, which propelled John Kerry to the presidential nomination.

Attending an event co-attended by the two Clintons, I wearily plunked myself into a chair. I didn't realize that my bottom had penetrated the inner sanctum of the VIP room.

Bill arrived first. Looking thinner, paler and older than I'd ever seen, the result of a heart ailment for which he'd soon undergo a quadruple bypass, he set himself up at one end of the VIP room, inches from me. He brightened as he posed for pictures with pretty girls, and signed copies of his memoir, *My Life*, for giddy supporters.

Several minutes later, arriving separately, Hillary marched in.

Immediately, she made a bee-line to Bill, moving her head in the direction of her husband's. And then I witnessed a bit of physical confusion that normally takes place between complete strangers.

Watching Hillary's face approach his, Bill apparently thought Hillary was about to give him a kiss. So Bill puckered his lips and shut his eyes. But he remained unkissed and looking silly. Hillary's face grazed past Bill's and settled by his ear, not his waiting mouth.

"That's John's brother," I heard her snap. Bill looked momentarily confused, opened his eyes, and shut his lips.

"John Kerry's brother!" she exclaimed impatiently. Hillary had walked over to tell Bill he must greet Cameron Kerry, the candidate's sibling.

Then she turned on her heel and walked away.

Bill returned to his book signing, his pictures with pretty girls. It was the only thing that made him smile. At one point, he even put his hand on my bare shoulder. Moments later, a Hillary staffer strode up and barked, "The Senator is ready when you are!" The Senator. I wondered, do these people know each other?

But Bill ignored her, and engaged in several more minutes of schmoozing before another staffer came over and said, more sharply, "She's ready!"

Finally, Bill reluctantly slunk out of the room and met his wife onstage with daughter, Chelsea. The couple linked hands. Hillary said, "Let me introduce you to Chelsea's father, a best-selling author, the man who taught the Democrats how to win again. A great, great president for the country to love ..." No mention that she was married to him.

I found myself feeling sorry for Bill as he told the crowd, "I want to say thank you for being so rowdy and irreverent and loud." Before the party, he said, "I felt pickled and old and half-dead—and you were having such a good time."

Then he pointed to his wife, the Senator, "She's the only one who can do anything for you anymore. She's got a real job."

Along the way, a funny thing happened. Hillary wore me out.

For so many years I had disliked this woman, despised her unnerving sense of entitlement. I wondered why having a cheating husband should grant anyone access to public office. Why Hillary?

I was not alone. The sputtering, undirected hatred from people like me had only served to make Hillary stronger. I believe she actually took comfort in my disdain. It was a known quantity, and it gave her focus. I had to declare it. I was done beating her up.

Around this time, Hillary announced that she would seek the presidency, not really a shock. She was fulfilling a promise she'd long ago made to herself, and her still-husband Bill: It was Hillary's turn.

I was forced to take a long, hard second look.

Well, she's certainly improved her look. And her talk. Years of practice and hard work had helped her on the stump to the point where I would give her a grade of "B." She'll never be as good as her husband—talent like that is inborn.

But what of it? Hillary has been around so long, made so many mistakes, it seemed unlikely she'd repeat them. She won't shove national health care down our throats again. She even voted with the Senate in favor of invading Iraq—it was the right thing to do at the time. Unfortunately, that vote handed Democratic opponent Barack Obama a blunt object with which to beat her about the head, in a war that had grown decidedly unpopular.

After a long look, I've come to this conclusion: Hillary is the devil we know.

In January 2008, she teared up on cue while campaigning in New Hampshire. Tears in New Hampshire sank the 1972 presiden-

> *After a long look, I've come to this conclusion: Hillary is the devil we know.*

tial campaign of Democratic Senator Edmund Muskie. But voters liked to see Hillary cry. She won the primary.

But in March 2008 came an even more telling moment.

"I remember landing under sniper fire," Hillary said about a visit to Bosnia as First Lady in 1996. "There was supposed to be some kind of a greeting ceremony at the airport, but instead we just ran with our heads down to get into the vehicles to get to our base."

Hillary's curiously detailed description of her heart-pumping Bosnia arrival immediately resulted in the appearance of videotape that demonstrated her landing in that country was entirely peaceful. In fact, she was greeted on the tarmac by a local child who read a poem. No bullets came close to Hillary's airspace. The military, responsible for Hillary's safety, was understandably perturbed at her insulting recollection. Bosnians, who cared for her, were furious.

Under fire now, for real, Hillary said she "misspoke" when recounting the danger. Of course, the Obama campaign helpfully produced three other examples in which Hillary "misspoke" about being shot upon, like some kind of latter-day Rambette.

There was no other explanation. It was a bald-faced lie intended to make the flailing candidate appear macho. And it was a lie from which Hillary would not recover.

A short time earlier, conservative commentator Rush Limbaugh made a fierce observation about Hillary, who'd turned sixty: "Will our looks-obsessed culture want to stare at an aging woman? Will this country want to actually watch a woman get older before their eyes on a daily basis?"

It was devastating to note that Hillary, the energetic survivor, had grown far from the Wellesley prodigy. She was Grandma.

I confessed in a column that I actually pulled the lever for Hillary on Primary Day in New York—yes, I'm a Democrat who frequently votes Republican. I'm as shocked as anyone. But I had no choice.

I'm not so naïve as to believe that politics has anything more than a passing acquaintance with public service, or even something as basic as truth. It is rather a sales job, in which candidates sell us on how they believe we should think and feel, not only about our country, but ourselves. What a load of BS.

I made a mental note to cancel out my primary vote for Hillary by choosing the Republican in the general election.

22

Sharpie and Shifty

THE REVS. AL SHARPTON
and JESSE JACKSON

That's all Hymie wants to talk about, is Israel; every time you go to Hymietown, that's all they want to talk about.

—The Reverend Jesse Jackson to the *Washington Post*, 1984

White folks was in caves while we was building empires... We taught philosophy and astrology and mathematics before Socrates and them Greek homos ever got around to it.

—The Reverend Al Sharpton at Kean College, 1994

THEY CAN BE as wickedly entertaining as they are wicked—the self-appointed civil-rights rock stars of the age. This pair will stop at nothing, not racist whites, not skeptical blacks, not even poorly maintained hotel room service, to get their faces on the six o'clock news. With their traveling dog-and-pony shows and well-practiced *schtick*, each man pops up at the drop of an "N-word," anywhere on the map, in time for deadline. They practically mutilated one another in 2007 to be first to arrive in Jena, Louisiana, to protest charges, including attempted murder, unjustly leveled against six black youth accused of beating a white student who'd hung nooses on a tree. But a black police officer murdered on the job by blacks rarely makes for a sexy cause.

That two such clownish figures could lay claim to being the leading civil-rights leaders of the day, supposedly walking in the footsteps of Dr. Martin Luther King Jr., speaks to the void that exists in the higher echelons of the movement.

What do they do for a living? These men may be ordained members of the cloth. But they represent organizations that seem to exist primarily to give them national platforms, for good or for ill.

Jackson ran for president in 1984, winning primaries in Louisiana, the District of Columbia, South Carolina, Virginia and Mississippi, then ran again in 1988, winning more. But he will forever be remembered as the man who referred to New York City as "Hymietown," a comment that revealed the gulf that exists between Jews and blacks, and the gulf that sits between Jackson's ears: He thought the reporter to whom he made the slur, Milton Coleman, would maintain his silence because he was black, too. With that single word, Jackson's political career evaporated overnight. I'd like to see Jesse Jackson win over primary voters in Crown Heights, Brooklyn.

Losing the trademark gold medallions, crazy bouffant hairdo and ample gut with which he rocketed to fame in the 1980s, a slimmed-down, besuited Sharpton ran for mayor of New York City and sought the Democratic nomination for president in 2004. With his quick wit and acid tongue, he made a few converts, and as many enemies. Try as a he might, he can't run from his support in 1987 of Tawana Brawley, a case that made, and ended, Sharpton's legitimate political career.

These days, I've made my peace

Try as he might, he can't run from his support in 1987 of Tawana Brawley, a case that made, and ended, Sharpton's legitimate political career.

with the Rev. Knowing I will never in this lifetime agree with anything that comes out of his yap, he likes to poke fun at me during
the rare instances I cover his events. At least my criticism is a constant. In another life, Sharpton should have been a night club
comic. Heck, I'd even buy a ticket.

Alfred Charles Sharpton Jr. was born October 3, 1954, in Brooklyn, New York, to Alfred Charles Sharpton Sr. and Ada Sharpton.
His parents split when he was ten so his dad could pursue a relationship with his stepdaughter, Al's half-sister. His mother worked
as a maid, but depended on welfare to get by. At the age of four,
Sharpton preached his first sermon. At nine, he was a licensed Pentecostal minister, but later became Baptist. Al Sharpton attended
Brooklyn College, dropping out after two years. He was a tour manager for James Brown in 1971 when he met his wife, backup singer
Kathy Jordan. They split in 2004, and have two daughters.

Sharpton got his first shot at the spotlight in 1986, when three
African-American men were chased by whites in Howard Beach,
Queens, onto the Belt Parkway, where one of the men was struck
and killed by a car. Sharpton, then in his track-suited, wildly
coiffed stage, became a national hero after leading 1,200 marchers
through the streets, while residents hurled racial epithets. It was
not Queens' finest moment. It was, however, Al's last great hurrah.

The next year came the fiasco which will be carved onto his
tombstone: The Tawana Brawley affair.

Brawley was a fifteen-year-old African-American girl from
Wappingers Falls, New York, with a story to tell. After going missing for four days, she was found smeared with feces and lying in a
garbage bag near her apartment, her clothes burned and torn and
racial slurs written over her body in charcoal. She said that six men
attacked her, raped her, and held her hostage. At least one of them,
she said, was a police officer. For Sharpton, it seemed too good to
be true.

Well, it wasn't.

Brawley ran away, a grand jury concluded after seven months of investigation, probably because she feared being beaten by her mother and stepfather for skipping school to visit her boyfriend in jail. She was seen at a party during the period she was "missing," and was witnessed crawling into the garbage bag herself. The racial slurs, written upside-down on her body, were likely written by Brawley.

But Sharpton simply refused to accept that his icon for racial savagery was slipping through his hands. He ratcheted up the volume, accusing Dutchess County prosecutor Steven Pagones, an innocent man, of being a "rapist" and "racist." Brawley, who has converted to Islam, has never spoken about it.

All Pagones got for his pain and suffering was a 1998 judgment of $345,000 against Sharpton and attorneys Alton Maddox and C. Vernon Mason. Sharpton dragged his feet over forking out his $65,000 portion, claiming he just couldn't afford it.

Can't afford it?

In an eye-opening 2000 deposition in the lawsuit, Sharpton testified that he owns not a single suit of clothes or television set, silverware or stereo, nor does he have access to a bank account. These things and more are provided for his use by his production company, Rev. Als Productions, and by the organization that has fed him for years, the National Action Network. Even more tricky, Rev. Als paid the $30,000 tuition bill for his daughters' private school, not a legally kosher move.

It all went away in 2001, though, when friends including Johnnie Cochran paid the $65,000 judgment to Pagones, who remains bitter to this day. Who can blame him?

Twenty years later, Sharpton said if he had to do it over again, he still would have taken the Brawley case—but he would not have made it personal against Steven Pagones. Too late, Rev. Too late.

Sharpton remains among the most polarizing figures of the day, though he's claimed to have mellowed after he was stabbed in the chest by a drunken white man in 1991 while preparing for a march in Bensonhurst, Brooklyn, over the killing of black youth Yusuf Hawkins. Mellow? That's an unlikely adjective, when you consider Sharpton's actions during one of the ugliest incidents in city history, the Crown Heights riots in 1991. It was the event that spelled the end to the one-term mayoralty of David Dinkins. Too bad reverends can't be impeached.

The riots started after a seven-year-old Guyanese boy was tragically—and accidentally—killed by a car driven by a Lubavitch Hasidic Jew. Riots by black residents of Crown Heights raged for four days, as the mayor fiddled. Stores were looted. Jews were trapped in their houses or beaten on the streets. Members of the mob shouted "Heil Hitler!" toward the Lubavitcher headquarters on Eastern Parkway. A moment of welcome levity arrived when *New York Newsday* columnist Jimmy Breslin was pummeled and stripped down to his underwear by the mob, then proceeded to file a column by telephone.

On the first evening of destruction, a Hasidic scholar visiting from Australia, twenty-nine-year-old Yankel Rosenbaum, was murdered—stabbed and beaten to death. When all was over, Jews rightfully called the riots a "pogrom." It was the darkest episode of anti-Semitism we'd seen in this country for quite some time. An utter disgrace.

Days after the dust settled, Al Sharpton did further damage to the shattered city's psyche when he led 400 protestors through Crown Heights. He led the mob in chants: "Whose streets? Our streets!" And, "No justice. No peace!" Mellow? No. Shameful? Yes.

Sharpton would like the city to forget his role in the arson and murder committed at Freddy's Fashion Mart in Harlem in 1995.

Sharpton would like the city to forget his role in the arson and murder committed at Freddy's Fashion Mart in Harlem in 1995.

It started after a black Pentecostal

church, which owned commercial property on 125th Street, planned to ask its Jewish tenant, the owner of Freddy's Fashion Mart, to evict a black sub-tenant who operated a record store. The record store owner did not take his eviction lightly. He called Sharpton, who promptly blamed not the church, but the Jewish man who operated Freddy's.

Sharpton made yet another statement that should forever be imprinted on his tombstone: "We will not stand by and allow them to move this brother so that some white interloper can expand his business."

After listening to this bunk for two months, a protestor, Roland J. Smith Jr. went into the store with a gun—shot three whites and a Pakistani—mistaking him for a Jew. He then set a fire that killed five Hispanics, one Guyanese and one black security guard whom the protestors derided as a "cracker lover." Smith also died. Sharpton, by the way, was not found legally culpable for the massacre.

In the aftermath of the Freddy's bloodshed, Sharpton sued the *New York Post* and myself for $20 million in 2000. He was upset that I called him a "carpetbagger from New Jersey" as he prepared to run for mayor of New York City. (He had relocated from Teaneck, New Jersey, to a house in Brooklyn.) He also sued over an editorial that reminded readers of the deadly arson at Freddy's, which he insisted was not his fault.

The suit was dismissed, with the judge pointing out the obvious: Sharpton had, in fact, lived in New Jersey. As for the fire, the judge said that whether Sharpton is "complicit" in the deaths in Harlem "is a matter of judgment, not of verifiable fact." Sharpton never made it to elective office.

Much later, he said he regretted the "white interloper" remark. Too late for that.

A strange sideline evidently enjoyed by Al Sharpton was that of FBI informant. The hobby was unearthed in 2002, just in time to cast aspersions on his run for president.

Sharpton was seen in a 1983 videotape discussing a drug deal with a Mafioso, who wanted Sharpton to introduce him to boxing promoter Don King. It was a sting meant to leverage his cooperation in bringing down people from the "movement." But Sharpton insists—hello!—that he's a victim here. He contended that a second tape existed that would exonerate him. He also denied acting as an informant on other occasions, including trying to arrange for the capture of cop-killer Joanne Chesimard, aka Assata Shakur, in Cuba.

Sharpton got big-mouth Don Imus fired from his gig at CBS radio for calling Rutgers women's basketball players "nappy headed 'hos," after Imus stupidly appeared on Sharpton's syndicated weekly radio program. Imus was simply no match for the slick-tongued Rev. Weirdly, the event has elevated Imus as an icon for freedom of speech, and he signed a new big-bucks contract with ABC radio.

The Rev. received a boost in stature from Mayor Michael Bloomberg. For eight years, Mayor Rudy Giuliani banished Sharpton from City Hall. He simply was not relevant. Whine as Sharpton might, few people, save for his diehard disciples, paid any mind. But Bloomberg brought Sharpton back to the table. Now, he's back as a constant on the scene. He held marches for the loved ones of Sean Bell, an unarmed black man shot to death tragically—and mistakenly—by panicky police officers, all of them minorities. Sharpton did not see it as an accident. Too bad he has little credibility.

JESSE LOUIS BURNS was born October 8, 1941, in Greenville, South Carolina, to a sixteen-year-old single mother, Helen Burns. His father, former boxer Noah Louis Robinson, was married to another woman and was not involved in his son's life. Jesse took the last name of his stepfather, Charles Henry Jackson.

Nearly sixty years after his birth, Jackson would admit that, while married, he fathered a child out of wedlock by a staffer of the charity he heads. Controversy arose when it was revealed that Jackson's Rainbow/PUSH Coalition, a tax-exempt charitable organization, paid the woman, Karin L. Stanford, enough to pay off a $365,000 house in Los Angeles. Charity officials insist this was not "hush money" but a legitimate business expense.

"I fully accept responsibility and I am truly sorry for my actions," said Jackson, who ironically counseled President Bill Clinton about his own extramarital dalliances. I'd like to be a fly on the wall for those sessions.

Did Jackson embellish the reason he transferred from the University of Illinois to North Carolina A&T? He claimed he moved because the racist school wouldn't let him play quarterback on the football team. But Illinois' starting quarterback that year was African-American. Jackson was, however, placed on academic probation just before he left.

Jackson was ordained a minister in 1968. His reputation as a civil-rights leader was cemented that year, when the young man happened to be with Dr. Martin Luther King on a Memphis balcony the day he was assassinated. His power base would eventually grow into the Chicago-based Rainbow Coalition, later Rainbow/PUSH, best known for pursuing headline-grabbing causes that give maximum exposure to its leader. Dr. King he is not.

Jackson angered President Ronald Reagan in 1983 when, asking no one's permission and feeling none necessary, he practiced foreign policy by traveling to Syria to secure the release of captured American Navy Pilot Lt. Robert Goodman, who'd been shot down over Lebanon on a mission to bomb Syrian positions. However, when the mission was a success, and Goodman came home Reagan made peace with Jackson and honored him. In 1984, he negotiated the release of twenty-two Americans held in Cuba by President Fidel Castro. These feats helped cement Jackson's credibility as a political leader, propelling his campaign to the nation's highest office.

It wouldn't last.

Jackson has been known to bop around the country in search of a cause. Some of them are disturbing: He visited with the parents of Terri Schiavo, the brain-damaged Florida woman whose parents tried in vain to keep her alive at all costs, despite fierce opposition from the woman's husband. Eventually, she died, but not in peace. Jackson also supported the North Carolina woman who falsely claimed she was raped by three Duke University lacrosse team players.

Jackson has lent his support to a movement to remove the so-called "N" word from the entertainment industry. And yet, the cry for banning the offensive word has been directed mainly at the media companies (usually white owned), and not the artists who embrace the word.

Even a broken clock gives the right time twice a day. Jackson has lent his support to a movement to remove the so-called "N" word from the entertainment industry. And yet, the cry for banning the offensive word has been directed mainly at the media companies (usually white owned), and not the artists who embrace the word. When do adults have to take responsibility for their actions?

Jackson, once a formidable figure, these days can be found at any high-profile trial involving a famous person. Even Michael Jackson.

I last saw Jesse Jackson in Santa Maria, California, during Michael Jackson's trial on charges of child sexual molestation. (The California jury acquitted him.)

That day, Jesse Jackson was wandering the streets aimlessly with a half-dozen members of his entourage, telling anyone who asked, and a few who did not, that he'd prayed with the singer. He was such a constant figure at the trial, the media quickly wearied of him. Even the local coffee shop where reporters regularly hung out ran out of seats for Jackson's crew.

Sadly, Jesse Jackson seems to have missed the memo that said the pop star he supported had long before turned against not only his black skin, but his male gender. Still, I found myself feeling a little sorry for the once-in-demand Jesse Jackson, so I asked him a question or two. I can't for the life of me remember what he said.

It was a slow day.

23

Pe-lousy

NANCY PELOSI

CELEBUTARDS AND DUMB foreign policy go hand-in-hand, like super-models and laxatives. Nancy Pelosi is no different. A mother of five who was elected to Congress from San Francisco in 1987, she was named House Speaker ten years later, the first woman to hold the title. Katie Couric cheered.

Against the wishes of the White House, the new speaker joined her comrades for a 2007 Middle Eastern tour. Question: What do you get when you cross a pushy and naïve San Francisco liberal with Arab leaders on a charm offensive? Answer: An international embarrassment.

Pelosi was born Nancy Patricia D'Alesandro on March 26, 1940, in Baltimore, Maryland. When her fifth child entered high school, the millionairess housewife (husband Paul's $25 million comes from real estate and investments) took to politics like Michael Moore to an organic buffet, hop-scotching up the Congressional ladder, from minority whip and finally to speaker—third in line to the presidency.

Evidently, Pelosi believed she alone was capable of breaking the violent impasse between Israel and her Arab neighbors. So in 2007, she took off with a Congressional delegation that included two

Republicans, visiting Israel, Syria, the Palestinian territories, Lebanon and Saudi Arabia.

In Syria Pelosi was captured in photographs she doubtless regrets, "going native" in an Arabic head scarf. She showed a lot of bare knee and hints of thigh while chatting with Syrian President Bashar Assad, in a land where women are advised to dress conservatively, or else.

After the meeting with Assad, Pelosi held a press conference in which she announced that she'd brought the Syrian leader a message from Israeli Prime Minister Ehud Olmert: Thanks to Nancy, Israel was ready to negotiate for peace! But Olmert had expressed no such thing.

His staff later clarified what Olmert actually said: "Although Israel is interested in peace with Syria, that country continues to be part of the axis of evil and a force that encourages terror in the Middle East."

Israel hinted at Pelosi's nefarious motives. "Pelosi took part of the things that were said in the meeting and used what suited her," Olmert's aides said. Can you spell "disaster"?

Later, visiting Saudi Arabia, Pelosi complained to officials about the lack of female politicians. As if that's the biggest problem facing the nation that produced Osama bin Laden.

To this day, Nancy Pelosi hangs on to the hope that peace is possible. And that Nancy Pelosi matters.

"The road to Damascus is a road to peace," she said. Whatever that means.

Inexplicably, on February 16, 2008, Nancy sent the House on vacation. She did so hours before the Protect America Act was set to expire without a House extension. The Senate found time to pass the ex-

Later, visiting Saudi Arabia, Pelosi complained to officials about the lack of female politicians. As if that's the biggest problem facing the nation that produced Osama bin Laden.

tension, and the House certainly had enough votes. But Pelosi was adamant that her people get an immediate break.

Never mind that the Foreign Intelligence Surveillance Act needed to be updated immediately. The law gives the government the ability to eavesdrop on foreign communications without warrants. As the bill hit the sunset, America's capacity to gather intelligence on terrorists overseas was badly compromised. We were in danger.

Pelosi's House used plenty of session time to explore in depth such matters of critical national import as steroid use in Major League Baseball. Now it was time for vacation, baby!

Where was the fire?

Townhall.com reported that Pelosi's daughter, Christine, was getting married on Valentine's Day weekend, and Mom was in a hurry to get to the wedding.

At least Nancy Pelosi brakes for traditional family values.

She topped herself on the last day of February 2008 when she pushed through the House a bill that would scrap some $18 billion in tax deductions given to American oil companies, saying, "The big five oil companies recently reported record profits for 2007."

But with this bill, big oil would be deprived of money used for developing new sources of supply, and certainly result in raising the already sky-high price of gasoline. And Pelosi failed to mention that her pet legislation exempted Citgo. The oil company operated by the brutal leftist dictator Hugo Chavez would keep its six percent American tax deduction.

President Bush vowed to veto the bill if it somehow made it through the Senate. As if Congress had nothing bigger on its plate.

Nice going, Nancy the Red.

24

Dying Is Easy; Comedy Is Hard

BILL MAHER

☆

WHEN BILL MAHER'S ONSTAGE, comedy isn't too funny.

Comedian Bill Maher, born William Maher, Jr., on January 20, 1956, in New York City, most certainly believes in something. But what? Well, he believes in the legalization of marijuana and gambling, in gay marriage, and he also serves on the board of that celebutard-friendly group sometimes compared to a terrorist organization, People for the Ethical Treatment of Animals. Maher is a big believer in the dignity of animals. Humans, not so much.

Maher was famous as the host of *Politically Incorrect* on Comedy Central and ABC until the show was bumped from the tube following his tasteless broadcast on September 17, 2001. As smoke still rose from downtown New York where terrorists did their worst, Maher made the bloodthirsty attack into something worse than a joke. He applauded the bravery of the butchers.

"We have been the cowards lobbing cruise missiles from 2,000 miles away," he said. "That's cowardly. Staying in the airplane when it hits the building, say what you want about it, it's not cowardly."

This, from a man who had the deep sensitivity to compare dogs to mentally retarded children: "But I've often said that if I had—I have two dogs—if I had two retarded children, I'd be a hero. And yet the dogs, which are pretty much the same thing. What? They're sweet. They're loving. They're kind, but they don't mentally advance at all . . . Dogs are like retarded children."

He's called himself a libertarian. And yet, he kneeled with lefty, loony Michael Moore on the set of his new show on HBO, *Real Time with Bill Maher* to beg Ralph Nader to drop out of the 2004 presidential race to make way for John Kerry. Didn't work.

Making fun of religion is another major theme for Maher. On an August 2005 appearance on *Larry King Live*, a caller asked him, "Hi. Well, my question is, the Lord spoke to me approximately three years ago, and if the Lord spoke to you, I was wondering if you'd become a believer."

Maher didn't hesitate.

"No, I'd check into Bellevue, which is what you should do." Then he trashed all religions, particularly Scientology, as comparable to mental illness.

"Like all religious people [they] have a neurological disorder. And the only reason why people think it's sane is because so many other people believe the same thing. It's insanity by consensus."

A few days later, he told Larry King that Christian promises of life after death were like promises made by politicians to get elected.

> *In Maher's world, religion is sick, but child molestation is understandable.*

In Maher's world, religion is sick, but child molestation is understandable.

Appearing on Craig Ferguson's *Late Late Show* in May 2005, Maher excused Michael Jackson's habit of sleeping with little boys as not such a bad thing.

"I think that there is no perspective," said Maher. "People have no perspective, especially about crime. You know, zero tolerance. You know, of course, nobody ever wants to see a child, you know, diddled. That's just plain wrong. But even the people who are testifying against him, they're saying that he serviced them. They didn't service him."

Ferguson, who has a son (Maher does not) said the idea of a pervert touching his kid drives him crazy. Still, Maher persisted.

"Very wrong. But, you know, I remember when I was a kid. I was savagely beaten once by bullies in the school yard. Savagely beaten. If I had a choice between being savagely beaten and being gently masturbated by a pop star, I'd go with the masturbator. It's just me."

Ferguson abruptly ended the interview. He probably saved his guest from himself.

Who knows? Maher might next have mused approvingly about brave, gentle terrorists sexually abusing religious folk.

25

In the Sweet By and Bias

KATIE COURIC

SHE WAS THE REIGNING sweetheart of morning television. Then after her husband died of colon cancer, she tried hard news, undergoing a colonoscopy, live, on air, on NBC's *Today* show.

But this did not come close to another kind of rectal incursion Katie Couric underwent after she moved to CBS in September 2006, becoming the first woman to anchor a network evening news broadcast solo.

I wrote at the time: "Katie chose to wear an unfortunate white blazer—the result, no doubt of some jokester lying to her face when Katie asked, 'Does this make me look fat?' And the day after Labor Day, to boot!" Others were harsher.

And still, I could excuse any sartorial sins committed by Katherine Anne Couric, born January 7, 1957, in Arlington, Virginia, were it not for her maddening insistence on pushing her views under the guise of news.

Couric is a tiger when confronting enemies, such as National Rifle Association president Charlton Heston. But she is a silky kitten when faced with her idols, Hillary Clinton or Jimmy Carter. Displays of American patriotism make her run for the Maalox.

"Of course, he is considered by many as one of the finest former presidents this country has ever seen!" Couric gushed as Carter, the anti-Semite who kissed up to Venezuelan president and America-hater Hugo Chavez, received his 2002 Nobel Peace prize. "Once again, we send out our heartfelt congratulations to President Jimmy Carter!"

She suggested in 1999 that "Christian conservatives" were to blame for creating an atmosphere in which James Byrd and Matthew Shepard were lynched for being black and gay. She did not try to conceal her excitement as Nancy Pelosi was named House minority leader in 2002.

"Is it okay to say, 'You go girl?' " she asked Ann Curry. Ann ruled it okay.

Couric has repeatedly applauded France for being more family-friendly than the United States. "So great that young mother being able to come home at three every day and spend that time with her child. Isn't that nice? The French, they've got it right, don't they?" she said.

She went into conniptions when Domino's Pizza founder Tom Monaghan talked of building a community based on Catholic values in 2006. "You can understand how people would hear some of these things and be like, 'Wow! this is really infringing on civil liberties and freedom of speech and right to privacy and all sorts of basic tenets that this country was founded on.' Right?"

And she plagiarized a "Katie Couric's Notebook" column on the CBS News website, in which she fondly remembers getting her first library card. The rest was stolen from a *Wall Street Journal* piece about the decline of libraries. CBS deemed Couric innocent, but fired a producer.

That notebook also screwed up a story about Barack Obama, provocatively titled, "Is America ready for a president who grew up praying in a mosque?" While I hold no love for Obama, I must say this lousy piece of journalism was based on the recollection of a childhood friend who initially said he saw Obama praying in an Arab temple—but later said he didn't think so. CBS took the piece down. They did not take down Katie.

Couric managed to anger her natural allies on the left with her snooze-worthy reporting from Iraq, to which CBS sent her in a desperate bid to shore up bottom-feeding ratings. Or maybe the network was employing a passive-aggressive method for finding a new anchor?

COURIC MANAGED TO anger her natural allies on the left with her snooze-worthy reporting from Iraq, to which CBS sent her in a desperate bid to shore up bottom-feeding ratings. Or maybe the network was employing a passive-aggressive method for finding a new anchor? MoveOn.org slammed her for doing "puff pieces" dictated by the Bush administration. It mattered little. Her ratings tanked.

SHE ANGERED EVERYONE ELSE, and threw away any remaining shred of journalistic integrity, when she told a National Press Club audience that it was "pretty much accepted" that the war was a mistake.

"Everyone in this room would agree that people in this country were misled in terms of the rationale for this war," she said. Not an original thought. But where had Katie's objectivity gone?

She then bizarrely slammed the American patriotism on display in the days following September 11, 2001.

"The whole culture of wearing flags on our lapel and saying 'we' when referring to the United States and, even the 'shock and awe' of the initial stages, it was just too jubilant and just a little uncomfortable."

Couric admitted agreeing with Iranian President (and Jew, gay and America-hater) Mahmoud Ahmadinejad on one point. "Oftentimes Westerners don't really understand fully the values of this particular culture. And I think the jury is still out as to whether democracy can really thrive in Iraq."

So Katie Couric is made uncomfortable by expressions of patriotism. And she cribs from Ahmadinejad.

Need I say more? Katie Couric is the epitome of celebutardom. Fat funnyman Oliver Hardy once said, "The character I play on-screen is the dumbest kind of person there is—he's a dumb person who thinks he's smart."

You listening, Katie?

26

Domestic Dominatrix
MARTHA STEWART

☆

THE TV-WATCHING PUBLIC knows Martha Stewart as the "domestic diva," a freakishly exacting homemaker, magazine editor, saleswoman and host of an eponymous daytime TV show. But in 2004, the government added the titles "conspirator," "liar" and "obstructor of justice" to Stewart's name, as she was convicted in a federal trial that turned into a three-ring circus with the appearance of famous friends such as Bill Cosby and Rosie O'Donnell. Even actor Brian Dennehy showed up. He called Martha Stewart a "good broad."

I added to her moniker the title of "domestic dominatrix." No one bullies toadies and underlings as thoroughly as Martha Stewart.

Born Martha Helen Kostyra on August 3, 1941, in Jersey City, New Jersey, Martha risked the company she founded, Martha Stewart Living Omnimedia, in 2003 when she was advised by stockbroker Peter Bacanovic to sell her shares of ImClone stock. By selling, the billionaire magnate avoided a loss only of some $45,000.

Ironically, Martha was not charged with the sale, but rather with working diligently to cover up the deed, a crime that harms the integrity of the nation's stock market. At any point, Martha had an opportunity to simply admit what she did. She could have said, "I'm sorry," and walked away with barely a slap on the wrist.

Admit she was wrong? You don't know Martha Stewart.

Defiantly protesting her innocence to the end, she was convicted one cold day in New York of conspiracy, obstruction of an agency proceeding, and making false statements to federal investigators. Bacanovic was hit with convictions for perjury, conspiracy and making false statements.

The day she went down, Stewart, a chinchilla scarf draped around her neck, stepped out of the courthouse and said, "Today is a shameful day. It's shameful for me, and for my family, and for my beloved company, and for all of its employees and partners."

Her company is "beloved." And her family? Not so much.

"What was a small, personal matter became, over the last two years, an almost fatal circus event of unprecedented proportions. I have been choked and almost suffocated to death during that time, all the while more concerned about the well-being of others than for myself, more hurt for them and for their losses than for my own, more worried for their futures than the future of Martha Stewart, the person."

And then, the sales pitch—"Perhaps all of you out there can continue to show your support by subscribing to our magazines, by buying our products, by encouraging our advertisers to come back in full-force to our magazines."

A masterful performance. Martha Stewart, criminal, had transformed herself into a victim, and turned her guilty verdict into a business opportunity. She soon became richer than ever before. Message: Don't mess with a diva wielding garden shears.

Stewart insisted on immediately serving her five-month sentence in

Don't mess with a diva wielding garden shears.

the federal penitentiary in Alderson, West Virginia, rather than wait for appeals to go through. Brilliant. Nobody noticed when her appeal was denied.

Before she took off for the can, another billionaire ex-con, convicted tax cheat Leona Helmsley, passed, through me, these words of advice to Martha: Get along.

"I was a good girl," Helmsley revealed of her eighteen months as an inmate. "I got up early. I went to bed early. I obeyed everything they told me.

"If people are going to be contrary, there's really nothing that's going to help them. Darling, they're not there to torture you. They're there to reform you."

Helmsley's prison secret? "I gave someone a quarter," she chuckled, "so she made my bed."

Martha, who treats me with the warmth normally reserved for virulent diseases, did not say goodbye.

27

Raider of a Lost Art
STEVEN SPIELBERG

☆

STEVEN ALLAN SPIELBERG, born December 18, 1946, in Cincinnati, Ohio, has amassed Academy Awards, lavish praise and a net worth estimated at $3 billion as the feel-good director of appealing and highly moralistic films that exude affection for America (*E.T: The Extra-Terrestrial*) and his fellow Jews (*Schindler's List*). Perhaps Spielberg itched to be edgy. Or maybe he's spent too many years in Hollywood. But in 2005, he co-produced and directed a film—*Munich*—that made me question his values, his morals, his loyalties. And most of all, his intelligence.

The film concerns the 1972 massacre in Munich, Germany, of eleven Israeli Olympic athletes by Palestinian butchers. Leaving little question as to which side the movie would take, it features a screenplay co-written by Israel-hating Jew Tony Kushner, who describes the establishment of the Jewish state as a "mistake." Spielberg, not known for subtlety, drives home the point that Israel exists in error.

The film centers around members of the Mossad—Israel's secret police—assembled to assassinate the killers, one by one. But in the film, one by one, members of the Israeli hit squad suffer crippling crises of conscience. In one memorably annoying scene, an

Israeli hit man screams in agony: "All this blood cries back to us! Jews don't do wrong because our enemies do wrong. We're supposed to be righteous!" Mercifully, he soon blows himself up.

Munich reeks of dangerous moral relativism. Unprovoked murder by terrorists is portrayed as no worse a deed than revenge-seeking against unrepentant killers. Spielberg exerted his sense of moral outrage in 2008 when he bowed to Hollywood pressure and resigned as artistic director of the Beijing Olympics, complaining that China did too little to halt bloodshed in Darfur. If only his movie was so morally clear.

Spielberg told *Time* magazine, bizarrely, "A response to a response doesn't really solve anything." With that, Spielberg changed the nature of the atrocities committed in Munich from murder, to a "response." To what, exactly? He never said.

In the end, the demoralized leader of the Israeli hit team, Avner (played by Eric Bana), flees to Brooklyn. The head of Israel's Mossad (Geoffrey Rush) shows up and tries to lure him back into service, saying his actions will bring peace.

"There is no peace!" Avner wails. In the background, the twin towers of the World Trade Center are visible.

Is Spielberg issuing a ham-handed warning about America's response to the looming terrorist attacks of 9/11? "Revenge?" he seems to say. "Not such a good idea."

Last I checked Steven Spielberg does not make foreign policy. For that I am grateful.

28

Everybody Must Get Stoned
SHARON STONE

☆

WHAT TO DO IF YOU DISAGREE with your government? Write a letter? Stage a protest? Vote? If your name is Sharon Stone, you would
travel to the heart of the Islamic world and give an anti-American
earful to Saudi Arabia.

Stone, born Sharon Vonne Stone on March 10, 1958, in Meadville,
Pennsylvania, rocketed to fame by crossing and uncrossing her legs
and displaying her goodies in 1992's *Basic Instinct*. Her reputation
as a man-eater got a further boost on the day she famously fed ex-
husband Phil Bronstein's big toe to a Komodo dragon at the Los Angeles Zoo in June of 2001.

But sex kitten roles quickly grated on the starlet, who craved
being taken seriously. And yet, crashing into the public consciousness via celebutard-heavy Hollywood requires more strenuous
measures than flashing a peace sign at the Oscars or complaining
about the president. *Anyone* can do that.

To that end, Stone gave an interview to a newspaper owned by
citizens of Saudi Arabia—the country that spawned Osama bin Laden.
She said the September 11, 2001, terrorist attacks on the United
States should not have been used as a pretext to launch wars in
Afghanistan and Iraq.

"When we choose war, we should understand that we choose murder, bloodletting and torture," Stone dramatically told the newspaper, *Al Hayat*, while attending the fourth Dubai International Film Festival in the United Arab Emirates in December 2007. The paper published excerpts in February 2008. Its sister publication, *Leha*, eagerly printed the entire interview.

"I feel at great pain when the spotlight is on the death of 4,000 American soldiers, while 600,000 Iraqi deaths are ignored," Stone continued—using a number of Iraqi casualties that is widely considered to be vastly overstated. Nevertheless, "War is not a movie. It is a tragedy of dead bodies, victims, the disabled, orphans, widows and the displaced."

> *Stone told the Arab media, known for its biases, that she checked out the region because the media in her own country distorted the truth.*

Stone told the Arab media, known for its biases, that she checked out the region because the media in her own country distorted the truth.

"I feel sad when I realize how much truth is being changed or obscured in the American media," she said. She added that she disapproved of military conflict with Iran, saying the United States should rather negotiate with Tehran or enact a trade boycott and sanctions.

Stone further slammed both Arab nations and Israel for failing to resolve conflicts that have long raged in the Middle East. The answer, Stone suggested, is as simple as joining a twelve-step program.

The region is "addicted" to the status quo, she said vapidly, adding that hysteria takes over whenever a solution to violence is close at hand.

"People sometimes get used to their choices and they fear change," she said.

The noted Middle East scholar presumably kept her legs tightly crossed, so as not to offend.

Of course, Stone's hardened and loopy spiritual principles can be bent, for a price. Stone was dropped as Christian Dior's China pitchwoman, when she remarked, bizarrely, in May 2008 that the killer earthquake that decimated parts of China may have been the result of "bad karma" over China's treatment of Tibet.

The actress issued a groveling apology, as she tried to save her lucrative ad campaign. "Due to my inappropriate words and acts during the interview, I feel deeply sorry and sad about hurting Chinese people," she said.

The *Xinhua News* agency dubbed Stone the "public enemy of all mankind."

That karma's a real bitch.

29

The Left Wing

MARTIN SHEEN

☆

BORN RAMON GERARDO ANTONIO ESTEVEZ in Dayton, Ohio, on August 3, 1940, the actor known as Martin Sheen shot to fame for starring in 1979's *Apocalypse Now*. But his helmet hair, not his vertically challenged stature, has typecast him for decades in roles as politicians and presidents. He portrayed both President John F. Kennedy (in the 1983 TV miniseries *Kennedy—The Presidential Years*) and his brother, Attorney General Robert F. Kennedy (in the 1974 TV special *The Missiles of October*). He was White House Chief of Staff A. J. McInnerney (in the 1995 flop *An American President*), and creepy future president Greg Stillson (in 1983's *The Dead Zone*).

Finally, he played popular liberal President Josiah Bartlet in the TV series *The West Wing*—in which he proved incapable of correctly pronouncing the capital of his supposed home state of New Hampshire, Concord. (Any New Hampshire resident will say Concord is pronounced like "conquered"; Sheen insisted on putting stress on the first syllable, like the grape.) But never mind. According to the show, we're supposed to believe that a lefty Eastern academic could be elected to the White House, too.

Sheen is not like Josiah Bartlet. He's far to the left. Fortunately, the actor, who's never attended college, has resisted calls to run for office. "You can't have a pacifist in the White House," he said. "I'm an actor. This is what I do for a living."

Fortunately, the actor, who's never attended college, has resisted calls to run for office.

That did not stop Sheen from being named honorary mayor of Malibu, California, in 1989. Promptly, he kookily proclaimed the town "a nuclear-free zone, a sanctuary for aliens and the homeless, and a protected environment for all life, wild and tame." The Malibu Chamber of Commerce considered revoking his title, but chose not to.

Sheen has lent his face to myriad causes, including the anti-Iraq War sleep-in outside President Bush's ranch in Texas by celebutard Cindy Sheehan. "At least you've got the acting president of the United States," he cracked.

But Sheen far outdistanced himself from the wacky Hollywood pack in October 2007, when he agreed publicly with his actor son Charlie Sheen's theories that the September 11, 2001, terrorists attacks were an inside job.

"Up until last year I was very dubious," he said at a Los Angeles anti-war rally. "I did not want to believe that my government could possibly be involved in such a thing. I could not live in a country that I thought could do that—that would be the ultimate betrayal. However, there have been so many revelations that now I have my doubts, and chief among them is [World Trade Center] Building 7—how did they rig that building so that it came down on the evening of the day?"

How indeed? I wish Sheen would return to fighting genocide in Darfur, Sudan, a more appropriate celebutard cause.

But then, that hobby is not as sexy as accusing the government of conspiring in the mass murder of Americans.

30

Curious George

GEORGE SOROS

HE'S BEEN CALLED the "Daddy Warbucks of drug legalization." He's also been dubbed a Jewish anti-Semite. And a threat to democracy.

George Soros, who made billions as a hedge fund operator, has financed untold numbers of political and social causes through his lavishly appointed Open Society Institute, an organization that quietly buys influence in the American way of life. Soros is well known for donating to Democrats and the radical group MoveOn.org. But less well publicized was his financing of rallies in favor of illegal immigration that seemed to "spontaneously" erupt around the nation in 2006. The apparent grass-roots nature of the protests clearly had the desired impact on public policy, persuading fence-sitters that illegals were here to stay. Little did we know that George Soros was the Wizard of Oz pulling the strings behind the curtain.

He was born August 12, 1930, in Budapest, Hungary, as Gyorgy Schwartz. His family changed its name in 1936 to the non-Jewish sounding Soros because of rising anti-Semitism in Europe. Soros has said he grew up in a "Jewish, anti-Semitic home." Some things never change.

Soros came to the United States by way of London, founding Soros Fund Management and co-founding the Quantum Fund, which made him incredibly wealthy. And willing to share: PBS estimated he's given away $4 billion.

But he's not above making a buck at others' expense. He was called the "Man who broke the bank of England" after he sold short $10 billion-worth of pounds in 1992, making a billion in the process, and prompting a devaluation of the pound sterling. Malaysian Prime Minister Mahathir bin Mohamed called Soros a "moron" for weakening Asian economies through currency speculation. He was convicted of insider trading in France, but paid only (to him) a small fine.

Soros established himself as a self-hating Jew when he said at a 2003 forum in New York that the administrations of President Bush, Israeli Prime Minster Ariel Sharon—and oddly, himself—are to blame for renewed anti-Semitism.

"There is a resurgence of anti-Semitism in Europe. The policies of the Bush administration and the Sharon administration contribute to that. It's not specifically anti-Semitism, but it does manifest itself in anti-Semitism as well. I'm critical of those policies . . . If we change that direction, then anti-Semitism also will diminish . . .

"I'm also very concerned about my own role because the new anti-Semitism holds that the Jews rule the world . . . As an unintended consequence of my actions . . . I also contribute to that image."

Soros's organization paid some $720,000 to aid the head of NASA's Goddard Institute for Space Studies, James Hansen, who claimed in interviews that the U.S. government had "censored" his belief that global warming was an imminent threat. But the Soros connection somehow ended up on the cutting room floor, *Investor's Business Daily* reported in 2007.

It's stunning to see how many moves aimed at protecting Americans from terrorists have been scrapped or postponed, thanks to Soros' magic money.

It's stunning to see how many moves aimed at protecting Americans from terrorists have been scrapped or postponed, thanks to Soros's magic money.

Soros provided cash to the move to ban military tribunals against enemy combatants held at Guantanamo Bay, Cuba. These were struck down by the U.S. Supreme Court in 2006. He also pushed the Transportation Security Administration to dump "Secure Flight," recommended by the 9/11 Commission—which matched airplane passenger lists with the names of known terrorists. Due to the invasion of privacy it presented, the program was suspended in 2006.

He was a key financial supporter behind the 2008 presidential campaign of Barack Obama, who took his dough even after Soros compared the Bush Administration to the Third Reich. "America needs to follow the policies it has introduced in Germany," he said. "We have to go through a certain de-Nazification process."

But his pet project remains the legalization of marijuana, a cause to which he's dropped millions. It's led James Califano, Jimmy Carter's secretary of Health and Human Services, to blast him as drugs' "Daddy Warbucks."

Soros insists there's nothing wrong with trading money for political influence.

Certainly, $4 billion—and counting—buys a lot of juice.

31

Shadow of a Dowd
MAUREEN DOWD

☆

MAUREEN DOWD, the Pulitzer Prize-winning *New York Times* op-ed columnist and author (*Are Men Necessary?*) has a guy problem.

Born January 14, 1952, in Washington, D.C., Dowd's writing is littered with cutesie nicknames (President Bush the first is "Poppy," Vice President Dick Chency is "Darth"). But Dowd officially joined the confessional, chick-lit genre by penning two astonishingly passive-aggressive pieces in the wake of failed relationships with producer Aaron Sorkin and movie star Michael Douglas, who took flight after meeting Catherine Zeta-Jones, whom he later married.

Rather than take out her anger on those who dismissed her, Dowd trained her high beams on *New York Times* colleague Judith Miller. She also discovered a new primate to take the place of unreliable men: bonobo chimps.

First, the chimps.

In a 2002 column Dowd, who has not married, moaned that she's too powerful and accomplished to nail a man. Never mind that other powerful, accomplished women have mates. Dowd was the victim in her tale.

Apparently, human males would not do. So Dowd traveled deep

into the animal kingdom to find the bonobo—a being of sexual superiority.

"Because in bonobo society, the females are dominant," she wrote. "Just light dominance, so that it is more like a co-dominance, or equality between the sexes. 'They are less obsessed with power and status than their chimpanzee cousins, and more consumed with Eros,' *The Times's* Natalie Angier has written.

" 'Bonobos use sex to appease, to bond, to make up after a fight, to ease tensions, to cement alliances. . . . Humans generally wait until after a nice meal to make love; bonobos do it beforehand.' "

Dowd concluded, approvingly, about our malodorous cousins: "The males were happy to give up a little dominance once they realized the deal they were being offered: all those aggressive female primates, after a busy day of dominating their jungle, were primed for sex, not for the withholding of it."

Before moving permanently into the jungle, Dowd, in 2005, went off the rails in a highly personal excoriation of Judith Miller, the Pulitzer-winning reporter and alpha female who retired under a cloud after reporting claims, which turned out to be false, about Iraq possessing weapons of mass destruction.

"I've always liked Judy Miller," Dowd began. Mee-ouch! Judy was in trouble.

Dowd launched into her co-worker, writing about her "tropism toward powerful men"—an allusion to rumors of Miller's active premarital love life. Dowd was angry, but not about Miller's flawed reporting. She was still steamed about an incident that happened years earlier, in which Miller had the temerity to ask Dowd to give up her seat at a Washington press briefing.

"It was such an outrageous move, I could only laugh," Dowd wrote furiously.

Miller told me about Dowd over breakfast in New York a few years ago. "I used to think of her not as a friend, but as somebody I like. You see, I wasn't part of that inner girl gang.

"My problem is I'm too undiplomatic. I'm too blunt. But I like her, and I admired her tremendously," she said, pointedly using the past tense. "That earlier work."

What about asking Dowd to give up her seat? Judy said, "I'm sorry I took her chair away. I was covering it and wanted to sit close. But I'm sorry. I'm sorry!"

Next, Dowd told Don Imus she loves me.

I'm afraid. Very afraid.

32

King of the Manny State
MICHAEL BLOOMBERG

About $7.50 an hour?
—Michael Bloomberg's response when I asked him to name
the minimum wage as he ran for mayor in August 2001.
(It was $5.15)

WHAT'S A BIG-CITY MAYOR to do when violent crime falls to levels
unseen since the days dinosaurs roamed the earth?

If you're two-term New York City Mayor Michael Bloomberg,
born Michael Rubens Bloomberg on February 14, 1942, in Boston,
you turn your adopted home town into a "Nanny State"—pushing
through a ban on smoking in bars and restaurants (not such a bad
thing, really), the removal of trans-fats from restaurant food (come
on), and discouraging women who give birth in city hospitals from
bottle-feeding their young. Thanks to Mike, taxes on a pack of
smokes are the highest in the nation, with some brands costing
more than ten dollars in your corner bodega. He also pushed through
the city Health Department a regulation requiring restaurants to
post calorie counts of each item on the menu, with chains such as
Starbucks and Dunkin' Donuts leading the way. You mean there's

400 calories in that "low-fat" blueberry muffin? Mayor Mike may have put me off eating for good.

Bloomberg, a card-carrying liberal Democrat, joined New York's moribund Republican Party because it presented a clear path to Gracie Mansion, where he's never lived; his own Manhattan townhouse is much nicer. He paid at least $73 million of a fortune he amassed as founder of the Bloomberg L.P. financial media empire to get elected mayor in 2001. For his 2005 re-election, despite only token opposition, he spent some $75.5 million, or about $100 a vote. His net worth was estimated at a spectacular $11.5 billion in 2008.

He took a mayoral salary of $1.00 a year. (I could make a smart-ass remark here such as he's being overpaid, but that's too easy.)

I should have seen it coming. When Bloomberg first ran for mayor in 2001, I asked him to name the minimum wage.

He didn't hesitate. "About 7.50 an hour?" he said.

The federal minimum wage, which New York followed, was $5.15. I should have taken it as a sign. And yet, I voted for him. Twice. Actually, if you saw the Democratic Three Stooges running for mayor, you'd understand.

His mayoralty has been marked with some wild successes—violent crime has continued to drop like a stone—and a few, egregious misses.

The Reverend Al Sharpton, who was banned from City Hall while Rudolph Giuliani was mayor, was seen, front and center, at the press conference.

He squandered four years of his reign championing the building of a football stadium for the New York Jets (who regrettably play in New Jersey) on Manhattan's West Side. Problem was, the project required lofty public financing and would have resulted in choking traffic in that already crawling part of town. But Mike can afford a private box from which to watch the games with his equally rich pals, not far from home! The idea died when two leaders in New York's state legislature—a Republican and a Democrat—rejected it. State Assembly Speaker Sheldon Silver was vocal in his disgust. "Am I supposed to turn my back on Lower Manhattan as it struggles to recover" from the terror attacks of 9/11. Silver said. "For what? A stadium? For the hope of bringing the Olympics to New York City?"

Not to be undone, Mike further demonstrated his disdain for folks who don't live in $50 million Manhattan townhouses when he proceeded to try like mad to shove through the state Legislature a "congestion pricing" measure. He sold it as a way to reduce traffic and pollution—not an issue with the precious stadium—and win federal dollars. Problem was, it meant charging drivers eight dollars to drive their cars into Midtown Manhattan. (Many drivers from New York's four outer boroughs, with which Bloomberg has only a nodding acquaintance, already pay more than that in tolls.)

The episode wound up revealing precisely how tone-deaf and out of touch the wealthy mayor was from the majority of New York citizens. Despite promised federal dollars, congestion pricing came with no guarantees that mass-transit fares would be reduced or hold steady for the little people, who no longer would be able to afford driving their cars. The move was nakedly aimed at pleasing rich residents of Manhattan, like the mayor, who don't drive anyway, or can easily afford the tax. But congestion pricing died an ignoble death in the State Assembly in April 2008. Despite the mayor's fervent cheerleading, it was so unpopular it failed even to come up for a vote. The word "elitist" was uttered a number of times by state politicians who killed off Mike's folly.

Bloomberg reached his tone-deaf zenith on November 27, 2006, when he turned his back on the city's police department in a time of crisis. Less than forty-eight hours after New Yorkers learned that police had shot an unarmed black man, Sean Bell, outside a sleazy Queens strip bar under the mistaken belief he had a gun—and before any witness statements could be assembled - Bloomberg made up his mind:

"I can tell you that it is to me unacceptable or inexplicable how you can have fifty-odd shorts fired," Bloomberg said at City Hall. He added, "But that's up to the investigation to find out what really happened."

Why have an investigation, when you've deemed the shooting unacceptable?

Making matters worse, Bloomberg said of Bell and his friends, "There is no evidence that they were doing anything wrong."

The Reverend Al Sharpton, who was banned from City Hall while Rudolph Giuliani was mayor, was seen, front and center, at the press conference. Police Commissioner Raymond Kelly, thrown for a loop by the mayor's premature blast, was momentarily speechless, later saying the mayor "is entitled to his opinion."

Bloomberg attempted to repair the damage by saying he only gave the armchair opinion of a "civilian." As if New York's essential commander in chief may lapse into the role of civilian when it suits him.

On April 25, 2008, the three detectives charged in Bell's shooting were acquitted of all charges—including manslaughter and reckless endangerment—by Queens State Supreme Court justice Arthur Cooperman, who concluded that prosecutors had failed to prove a crime was committed. Bell's shooting was a horrible, fatal mistake, but it was just that—a mistake. Egg on his face, Bloomberg was asked if he put the city in jeopardy when he prejudged the shooting. The mayor merely showed a flash of the irrational anger he has shown whenever his back is to the wall, but refused to answer the question.

Our regal mayor picked a side. Too soon.

33

Town Without Pity

BRATTLEBORO, VERMONT

☆

A COMMUNITY (even one in California) is not ordinarily designated a celebutard. But Brattleboro, Vermont (established 1887; 2000 census population 8,259), worked hard to make this list.

This sleepy town in southern Vermont, previously best known for its overpriced maple syrup, became the location in which people spontaneously began tossing off their clothes and walking around downtown stark naked. It started in 2005 when teens played hula-hoops in a parking lot in the buff. Before long, senior citizens took to walking around exposed.

"I'm concerned we don't know where [naked people] are going to strike," worried a local minister, the Reverend Kevin Horion.

After two years of wringing hands and other body parts—Vermont had no law banning public displays of naughty bits—town elders commanded the populace to cover up. It was just the precursor to Brattleboro's biggest insanity. Gosh, I miss the nudists.

On Primary Day 2008, as the state ushered in Barack Obama as its choice for Democratic candidate for president, the towns of Brattleboro and nearby Marlboro voted to indict President George Bush and Vice President Dick Cheney for unspecified crimes. As if the region hadn't more important things to worry about—schools and the economy for starters—residents spent months agonizing before finally deciding that if the pair ever dared set foot within these borders, they'd be arrested on sight. Vermont is the only state in the union in which Bush had thus far failed to step foot. You won't see him around these parts any time soon.

I guess from now on I'll have to buy my extortionate syrup in New York.

34

DISHONORABLE MENTION

☆

Other Folks Who Drive Us to Drink, but Don't Rate an Entire Chapter

Al Franken (born Alan Stuart Franken on May 21, 1951, in New York) took it upon himself to body-slam an elderly Lyndon LaRouche supporter who heckled former lefty presidential candidate Howard Dean during a New Hampshire campaign stop in 2004. Franken broke his trademark Coke-bottle glasses during the brawl. In his defense, Franken said he would have attacked a Dean supporter if he shouted at a Kerry rally. (No mention of Bush.)

"I got down low and took his legs out," Franken boasted about his smack-down of a senior. "I was a wrestler so I used a wrestling move."

The cops arrived, but did not know what to make of the dumb beating the old.

In 2008, he announced he was running for Senate from Minnesota, where he grew up, as a member of the Democratic-Farmer-Labor Party. Opponents are advised to come armed.

* * *

I could go on about the proud anarchist **Noam Chomsky** (born Avram Noam Chomsky on December 7, 1928, in Philadelphia). But I think this single quote criticizing the United States' invasion of Afghanistan in the wake of the 9/11 terrorist attacks crystallizes how the biggest intellectuals are the dumbest people: "Wanton killing of innocent civilians is terrorism, not a war against terrorism."

'Nuff said.

* * *

Dan Rather (born Daniel Irvin Rather on October 31, 1931, in Wharton, Texas) was unceremoniously booted from CBS News after forty-four years after he reported a damning 2004 story critical of President George W. Bush's Texas Air National Guard service record. Problem was, the report was based on forged memos so crude, a toddler could have executed them. For a while, Rather feigned repentance. But later, he shockingly told Larry King, "Nobody has proved that [the memos] were fraudulent, much less a forgery. The truth of this story stands up to this day." He also sued CBS for $70 million. Way to end a career.

* * *

Christine Amanpour (born January 12, 1958, in London) deserves a special place in our hearts for her stubborn, pandering, Arab-centric coverage of the Middle East for CNN. Her macho posturing while facing down tyrants (accompanied by her protective entourage) is to make one ill. Sorry. Try as you might, you can't make them love you.

* * *

Aaron Sorkin (born Aaron Benjamin Sorkin on June 6, 1961, in New York) admitted he wrote the boring romantic comedy *An American President* while locked in a hotel room smoking crack, before creating TV's *The West Wing* and squiring Maureen Dowd. And this man is a major influence to today's budding lefties.

★ ★ ★

Being liberal in Massachusetts is easy. If you're Senator **Ted Kennedy** (born February 22, 1932), so is driving drunk in Chappaquiddick, then running from the scene after your vehicle dunks into the drink, leaving a young lady, not your wife, to drown. He pleaded guilty to leaving the scene of an accident, and spent not a minute behind bars. Last I saw Captain Oldsmobile, it was weeks after his son, Representative Patrick Kennedy, crashed his car on Capitol Hill. A cop said the rep appeared drunk. He insists he was on medication. Being a Kennedy, he pleaded to a wrist-slap offense of driving under the influence of prescription meds. When I caught up with Teddy K, he was in New York promoting a children's book about a black Portuguese water dog named—are you ready?—*Splash*. I could not invent this stuff. Ted was diagnosed with a malignant brain tumor in May 2008, though he did manage to make an appearance at the Democratic National Convention on opening night, August 25, 2008. If nothing else, it proves beyond doubt that a fatal disease is the only surefire cure for a bad reputation.

★ ★ ★

Woody Allen (born Allen Stewart Konigsberg on December 1, 1935, in New York) wrote an astonishing piece in the *New York Times* in 1988 urging his fellow Jews to exert "moral, financial, political pressure" against Israel to end oppression of Palestinians. But then, in 2002 he accused the American Jewish Congress for adopting Gestapo-like tactics—actually, his tactics. The AJC had urged a boycott of the Cannes film festival (where Allen's new movie coincidentally premiered) because of virulent French anti-Semitism. "Boycotts were exactly what the Germans were doing against the Jews," Allen told French radio. Why expect moral consistency from a man who incestuously married Soon-yi Previn, better known as the adopted daughter of Allen's girlfriend, Mia Farrow? When you're Woody Allen, morals are for other people.

★ ★ ★

Robert Redford (born Charles Robert Redford, Jr., on August 18, 1936, in Santa Monica, California) has an energy problem. The filmmaker and ardent environmentalist moans about administration failures to combat global warming and reduce the use of fossil fuels, while presiding over an SUV-locked Sundance Film Festival in Park City, Utah, several hours and many Lear jet rides away from the homes of anyone in the movie industry. John Tierney of the *New York Times* sensibly suggested that if Redford cared about the environment, he'd move his festival to New York, which would "spare [movie-makers] a trip, enrich our economy and save energy." Redford, however, persists in owning an environmentally unfriendly, remote and pricey ski resort.

★ ★ ★

Rob "Meathead" Reiner (born Robert Singer Reiner on March 6, 1947, in the Bronx, New York), a film director best known for playing Archie Bunker's son-in-law "Meathead" on the sitcom *All in the Family*, sponsored California's Proposition 10, which slapped a 50-cent tax on packs of cigarettes to pay for programs for children under five. *The Los Angeles Times* reported that 20 percent of the $700 million a year raised from the tax was spent on a "First Five Commission" run by, you guessed it, Rob Reiner. To that end, Reiner has awarded hundreds of millions to advertising and public-relations firms, in part to fund campaigns to pass new initiatives, including Proposition 82, which would have taxed high-earners for preschool. (It failed at the ballot box.) Reiner had to quit as head of the commission amid mounting criticism. Was this money well-spent? Or political patronage and waste levied by a rich liberal with little to do? You decide.

* * *

Jerry Seinfeld (born Jerome Seinfeld on April 29, 1954, in Brooklyn, New York) must ask his wife for permission to leave the house more often. Some questioned the faded '90s sitcom star's sanity in 2007, when he told David Letterman that a cookbook author was a "wacko" and potential serial killer. Why? Because many have suggested the author, Missy Chase Lapine, who wrote *The Sneaky Chef*—which tells how to hide pureed vegetables in kids' food—was plagiarized by Seinfeld's wife, Jessica, in her tome, *Deceptively Delicious*.

"Now you know, having a career in show business, one of the fun facts of celebrity life is wackos will wait in the woodwork to pop out at certain moments of your life to inject a little adrenaline into your life experience," Seinfeld said, comparing Lapine with Letterman's now-deceased stalker, as well as with a man who plotted to kidnap Letterman's son.

Like a tot on a sugar rush, Seinfeld noted Lapine used three names. "If you read history, many of the three-name people do become assassins," he said." Mark David Chapman. And you know, James Earl Ray. So that's my concern." Chapman gunned down John Lennon, but wrote no known cookbooks. James Earl Ray assassinated Martin Luther King Jr. and also never penned a cookbook.

* * *

Never having actually watched a program helmed by **Keith Olbermann** (born January 27, 1959 in New York), I am at a loss as to what gifts this influential (in his own mind) lefty has bestowed upon the universe. But Olbermann, who drew the ire of the Anti-Defamation League for repeatedly using the Nazi salute while referring to people he doesn't like, has nonetheless rewarded me. He named me his "Worst Person in the World" in 2006, after I reported on a loud conversation I overheard in which he envied Fox newscaster Bill O'Reilly's superior ratings, and guffawed as a pal scorned colleague Connie Chung as a death-defying "cockroach." Olbermann said that was meant as a "compliment." Thanks for keeping it real!

* * *

Some people get divorced. Others transform their lives and ideologies in the process of ridding themselves of a toxic spouse. **Arianna Huffington** (born Arianna Stassinopoulos on July 15, 1950, in Athens, Greece) says she was simply a "former right-winger who has evolved into a compassionate and progressive populist," as if such a shape-change overcame her during breakfast. She went from conservative to uber-liberal after her embarrassing divorce from former United States Senator Michael Huffington, who disclosed his bisexuality (a 1999 *GQ* profile declared that she knew of his sexual interest in men all along). Following the split, she became a wealthy woman from her ex's oil money, free to start the leftist online vanity sheet, The Huffington Post, which publishes the liberal musings of every manner of celebrity and deep thinker, from Alec Baldwin to Cindy Sheehan. Her biography on Maria Callas was the subject of a plagiarism scandal (settled out of court). These days, Huffington, with her charming accent and good hair, is a constant on the speaker's circuit, where leftists are in great demand.

And this book could not be complete without:

Jane "Hanoi Jane" Fonda (born December 21, 1937), the grandmother of the modern celebutard set, whose treasonous pose on an anti-aircraft battery in Hanoi during the Vietnam War in 1972 was credited by John McCain as earning him extra torture as a prisoner of war. In 2008, she used the word "c*nt," live, on the *Today* show while discussing her role in the *Vagina Monologues*—crudely and inadvertently crystallizing what so many have thought of her for decades.

INDEX